Wisdom from the Spirit World

Life Teachings on Love, Forgiveness, Purpose and Finding Peace

Wisdom from the Spirit World

Life Teachings on Love, Forgiveness, Purpose and Finding Peace

Carole J. Obley

**6TH
BOOKS**

Winchester, UK
Washington, USA

JOHN HUNT PUBLISHING

First published by Sixth Books, 2020
Sixth Books is an imprint of John Hunt Publishing Ltd., No. 3 East St., Alresford,
Hampshire SO24 9EE, UK
office@jhpbooks.com
www.johnhuntpublishing.com
www.6th-books.com

For distributor details and how to order please visit the 'Ordering' section on our website.

ISBN: 978 1 78904 302 0
978 1 78904 303 7 (ebook)
Library of Congress Control Number: 2019945733

A CIP catalogue record for this book is available from the British Library.

Design: Stuart Davies

UK: Printed and bound by CPI Group (UK) Ltd, Croydon, CR0 4YY
US: Printed and bound by Thomson-Shore, 7300 West Joy Road, Dexter, MI 48130

We operate a distinctive and ethical publishing philosophy in
all areas of our business, from our global network of authors to
production and worldwide distribution.

Contents

Other Works by Carole J. Obley

Books

Embracing the Ties That Bind: Connecting With Spirit (Xlibris, 2003; ISBN 1-4010-8971-2)

I'm Still With You: True Stories of Healing Grief Through Spirit Communication (6th Books, 2008; ISBN 978-1-84694-107-8)

Soul to Soul Connections: Comforting Messages From the Spirit World (6th Books, 2013; ISBN 978-1-84694-967-8)

Audio

Reconnect: Meditations for Healing (ISBN 24594-00602)
Igniting Your Spiritual Intuition, three-disc set with workbook (ISBN 84501-45384)

To Spirit,
in Its glorious Being and Forms;
and to all beautiful souls
residing on earth and in spirit.

Acknowledgments

I express my sincere gratitude to all who have contributed inspiration, support and assistance during the creation of this book. Certainly, no book is produced in isolation; we are all collaborators in life's journey. Specifically, I acknowledge the following contributions:

To Spirit, the Eternal One: You are the infinite source of wisdom, unconditional love and healing. Thank you for your gracious light, which can never be extinguished.

To my spirit guides, soul family and teachers: I could never adequately express how much your guidance on my pathway is appreciated.

To the souls in spirit who have communicated with me through thousands of sessions, giving countless messages and lessons about life, love, purpose and forgiveness: I express my humble gratitude for being a conduit for your thoughts and words.

To clients from all walks of life who've connected with me for readings, group mediumship and workshops: I am grateful for your presence and trust in me over the years. I could not do this without you.

To Gina Mazza: Your writing expertise and careful attention to detail during editing help bring clarity and refinement to my words.

To my husband, Jeff, my family and my dear friend, Alice: Your support of me has been truly unconditional.

To 6th Books: Thank you for accepting my manuscript so that it reaches those who will benefit from reading it.

To Embers, Phoenix and Cinders: I promise to continue studying the art of Zen, although I doubt I will master it as well as you.

Introduction

It's the final day of basic mediumship training at Delphi University in McCaysville, Georgia, and I'm required to give three readings to volunteers in order to graduate. Debra sits directly facing me in a small, secluded room. She smiles pleasantly as my mind races at the daunting task I'm about to do: give her a 15-minute reading. My thoughts silently scream endless uncertainties about my ability to perceive any relevant information to present to her. My heart pounds, my palms sweat. Thoughts of defeat swirl through my mind, making me dizzy.

How can I possibly do a reading for 15 minutes? What do I do if I can't tune into her? She seems like a kind person, but she's bound to laugh at me if I give her false information. Surely she'll get up and leave, or give me a negative review on the questionnaire she's been asked to fill out. I can't even remember what I was taught this week! Where do I begin? I can't do this! Help!

Finally, the moment comes. I'm on. Hesitantly, I begin to relay intuitive impressions to Debra as they slowly flow to me — most of which, to my surprise, she validates as I go along. I have doubts as to their accuracy but I take a deep breath and go with the impressions I'm receiving. Most of the insights concern Debra's career, relationship issues and upcoming decisions regarding a move. I train my eyes on the wall behind Debra to avoid being distracted by her reactions to my words. After a seeming eternity, the nearby timer dings, signaling the session's end. My stomach still churning with uncertainty, I direct my gaze at Debra to gauge her demeanor and reaction. A smile radiates on her face, giving me instant relief. *Whew! I made it through!* I stand up as she reaches out to hug me.

"How long have you been doing this?" she asks.

"Um, uh, well, you are my very first reading," I stammer.

"You're kidding! I would have guessed that you've been doing this for a long time," she responds. "Everything is so accurate!"

There's not a hint of insincerity in her voice. Dazed yet exuberant, I prepare for my second of the three "sitters" (as clients are called). *This isn't as hard as I thought it would be! One more reading after this one and I'm home free!* I would then be ready to graduate the next day and follow up at home with five readings to earn a gold seal on my diploma (a goal I would accomplish a month later).

Much has changed since that day more than two decades ago when I sat nearly frozen in front of Debra. In those beginning years, I didn't relay messages from sitters' deceased loved ones; these early sessions strictly dealt with earthly concerns like relationships, finances, health and career. A couple of years into mediumship work, messages from spirit beings began to unexpectedly permeate other types of psychic sessions I had been giving, including Tarot card readings. I'd be offering advice about a client's work when suddenly I'd receive an impression from one of their deceased loved ones. Over time, these "visits" and communications from spirit beings became more frequent during sessions. This propelled me to learn more about the mechanics of mediumship—how it operates, how to refine it and how to strengthen the connection with those in spirit. After earning my diploma from Delphi, I continued to train, take classes and hone my mediumship skills at Lily Dale in upstate New York, the largest center for **Spiritualism** in the United States.

Since then, I have been a conduit for those in spirit through more than 10,000 individual in-person and phone readings, as well as group and radio readings. In my wildest dreams, I couldn't have imagined back in my early years of training the clarity, specificity and, most importantly, the *healing* these sessions would bring to those who'd receive them. Yet as the years rolled on, I discovered that there was more depth yet to unfold in the readings. Remarkably clear details, descriptions and substantial evidence from spirit beings became the focus of the sessions. As even more time went by, I witnessed how these messages had profoundly uplifting effects on the recipients.

Early on, I also had no inkling about the illuminating spiritual lessons on life and death that those in spirit would communicate through me to their earthly families and friends. To say that I've learned so much from these benevolent beings is an understatement! Time and again, I've delivered messages with recurring themes about the continuity of life after death, the eternal nature of love, life priorities, the experience of death, painful generational patterns and, interestingly, soul lessons planned before birth (more on that later). These grace-filled pearls of wisdom were delivered in diverse ways: through direct, straightforward facts (teaching), **clairsentience** (feelings), humor and lightheartedness, as well as sincere regrets for missed opportunities during life. I've come to realize that although the flavor of delivery varies, the intent behind these messages is apparently the same: to offer spiritual guidance and healing for those in the physical world.

This includes me as the intercessor. Looking back, it's obvious to me that one cannot do mediumship work and not be profoundly changed by it. In the beginning, I was not aware of how much personal transformation this work would provide in terms of my spiritual growth. I am no longer the fearful, ego-driven person that I once was, thank goodness. I have grown in trust, faith and love because of my collaboration with Spirit. I've learned big lessons in humility, compassion, patience and determination. Granted, many times I've wanted to quit doing this work due to discouragement and burnout, but somehow, I've managed to stay the course for 24 years as of this writing. For all of these experiences, I am deeply grateful. Above all, I have grown immeasurably from listening to the inspiring wisdom that spirit beings have communicated during thousands of sessions. This timeless wisdom is the inspiration for this book.

Yet mediumship offers more than validation and insight about life's (and death's) deep mysteries; it also provides guidance in practically applying spiritual teachings to improve our earthly existence—individually and collectively. For instance, sitters often ask me why a particular issue arises or resurfaces in their lives—things like physical or mental illnesses, family drama, difficult relationships or the death of a child. That question is usually followed by another: *How can I successfully cope with this situation?* Messages delivered from the spirit realm shed light on these universal uncertainties, all from the elevated perspective of the soul. I share many of these insights in the upcoming chapters.

As with my previous three books, this one focuses on spiritual healing and the recognition of our true identity as eternal divine beings of love as perceived through the lens of mediumship. (To learn about the basics of mediumship and how it works, please see my book, *Soul to Soul Connections: Comforting Messages From the Spirit World.*) On these pages, we will explore the compelling knowledge, insight and counsel given by those who have (temporarily) completed their journeys in the physical world and returned home to the spirit realm. You will also be privy to wisdom imparted from my personal **spirit guides**, or souls in spirit who have agreed to help me with spiritual lessons during my earthly life.

In Part One, you will discover how the soul plans to experience life before taking physical form, including one's personal, unique challenges and the spiritual lessons needed to evolve. You will learn about the relationships that bring these lessons directly onto your path through **magnetic resonance**, or the "charge of attraction" that you have with other souls through relationships. I discuss my direct experience with and knowledge of the energetic imprints that souls carry from lifetime to lifetime (the

Akashic files). Also addressed here are helpful guideposts that you can use in your quest to recognize and decode your soul's imprinted lessons—also called **blueprints**—as you go about your life.

In Part Two, I relate various teachings on life and death that have been delivered by spirit beings during sessions. In all of my earlier books (listed in the back of this book), I shared true, unembellished transcripts of dialogue from private readings. In this book, I offer examples from my case study files along with composite examples that represent many readings with similar themes: the undying bond of love, forgiveness, regrets and priorities in life, for instance. It is my hope that you can more easily absorb the core of each teaching by reading these consolidated examples and dialogue.

Part Three offers simple, practical insights, recommendations and personal assessments to help you navigate life's challenging times and assist you in uncovering your unique strengths and life lessons. Here you will find roadmaps to chart your life with less pain, little resistance, and much more self-confidence as you unlock the treasure chest of your soul. For clarification of some of the key (boldfaced) terms used throughout the book, I've included a glossary with simple, concise definitions.

What strikes me most about what spirit beings have communicated is that we, as eternal souls, never cease evolving, both here and in spirit. They have often revealed that we alone are responsible for the quality of our lives. No one else can do what our unique soul has come to earth to do. Moreover, we experience planned challenges, hardships and heartaches in order to grow beyond our perceived limitations. Nothing we face in life is by chance. We can do the required work of these "plans" more easily by learning from the experiences, trials, regrets and rewards of those who have encountered the very same or similar experiences.

Through the real-life examples sprinkled throughout these chapters, you will marvel at how spirit beings eloquently communicate strength, wisdom and hope in coping with life's challenges. Their insights are truly a blessing for all and deserve to be shared. With a sincere desire to be of service, I offer a reiteration of them to the best of my knowledge and remembrance (based on actual sessions). May they inspire, uplift and transform your life in the most beautiful way. cjo

Part One

You Signed Up For This

One. Soul Maps and Karmic Lessons

Do not feel lonely; the entire universe is inside you.
~ Rumi

Marcia sits in front of me, her face flush from tears after hearing from her son, Jason, during our session. He had passed from a drug overdose seven months prior to our reading. Jason lovingly communicates specifics about his emotional state prior to ending his life: He'd been depressed after his girlfriend of five years broke up with him a few weeks after losing his job. Jason impresses on me that, at the time, he considered himself to be a victim of these painful life circumstances. He mistakenly thought that drugs (which he'd used sporadically for a decade) were the magic elixir for enduring the pitfalls in his life.

As the reading progresses, Jason's deceased grandfather (Marcia's father) appears to me through **clairvoyance** (perceiving beyond the physical world through inner sight) and speaks of his own addiction to alcohol, the havoc this caused in the family and how it plagued generations of Marcia's paternal lineage. He shows me a symbol of a thumb pointing backwards— an indication that the condition was present in previous generations. The grandfather impresses on me that he passed from the ravages of the disease, which corroded his liver and stomach. He mentions that he'd helped his grandson during his **life review**, a process that occurs once a person has transitioned from the body. (I discuss this experience in the next chapter.) I explain to Marcia that by helping Jason, the grandfather was likewise helping himself and all others in previous generations who had not healed from this condition.

"I don't understand why this happened!" Marcia blurts out. "I tried to help my son many times, but he ignored me and continued to use heroin. He'd disappear for days. I'd be up all night worrying about him. The last time I talked to him on the phone, he hung up on me because he said I was lecturing him and trying to control his life. I just can't get over losing him." She begins to sob. "I feel terribly guilty that I didn't do enough to save him, and I'm angry," she adds forcefully. "I'm angry that he did this to himself and to our family."

Her emotion is palpable, raw and painfully real. I pause before saying, "But this was not *your* choice, Marcia. Jason himself made the choice to use heroin. There was nothing you could have done differently than give him love as you did. In fact, you may have done *too* much as far as always being available to pick him up when he fell. In spirit, he now understands that the choices he made in life led to his untimely death and that he alone is responsible for them."

Marcia is silent as she absorbs this information. After a moment, I sense a slight flicker of acceptance brightening her awareness.

"I hope so because his death has just about killed me as well," she states flatly. "Why did this have to happen though? Why him, me, our family?"

She looks at me, her eyes frantically searching my face for the answer. In times of grief like this, experience has taught me that words offer little consolation. A similar scenario has played out during countless readings that I've given for those who've endured tragic losses such as the death of a young person. So I remained silent while Marcia processed through her emotions in those moments.

In addition to giving evidential messages from spirit beings, my primary intent is to help ease pain by sharing what I have learned firsthand as a medium: Although we don't recall doing so before birth, we plan deliberate challenges in our lives in order to grow and evolve spiritually. The reading with Marcia is an illustration of how these planned circumstances and events present us with opportunities to evolve spiritually through experiencing them. The choices we make when confronted with these challenges determine the quality of the next phase of our eternal lives—either on the physical plane or in the spirit world. Those choices rest solely with us.

Imagine floating high above the earth in a tranquil atmosphere. You are pure consciousness without a physical body. Blissfully drifting, you are unfettered by fears, concerns and problems. Pain is nonexistent. There is no past or future. Time is irrelevant. You are conscious only of being present. Other souls with whom you feel a deep resonance and unity encircle you. You have no recognition of those souls as individuals with personalities; you effortlessly blend and flow with one another, and they with each other. Relaxing waves of peace wash over you. In this limitless, expanded state, your soul recognizes its connection with all that is. It knows its own timelessness, eternity and oneness with the cosmic source of Spirit, the Father-Mother, the Source of all creation.

Now imagine you've become aware that you have further work to do that will ensure that you retain this memory of unity with Spirit forever. Something in your consciousness is not yet complete. Unfinished lessons of the soul are commonly referred to as **karma**, a Sanskrit word meaning "cause and effect." In short, what we create, we receive. Karma is one of the **natural laws**, a body of universal, immutable principles governing the consequences of human behavior. We work with karma during multiple incarnations as well as in between lives in the spirit world. Each experience is necessary in the process of our evolution and ultimately becoming one with Spirit. (For further information, check out *The Seven Universal Laws Explained* by Tania Kotsos at mind-your-reality.com.)

In the spirit world before you incarnate, faint memories of this unfinished work filter into your awareness as beings of high spiritual consciousness—your **guardian angel** (a divine being who is with you through many lifetimes), **master teachers** (beings who impress us with wisdom about spirituality and specific life lessons), and **spirit guides** (beings who help us on our earthly journey)—draw near. They do so to gently remind you that the time is at hand to decide what experiences and circumstances in the physical world will help you to remember your divine identity. This "panel" of wise beings is familiar with the lessons and experiences that your soul needs to spiritually evolve. Based on this knowledge, they impress upon you that they will help you plan your descent into the physical realm to continue your journey of spiritual evolution. Through intuitive awareness, you know their guidance is true. You agree to meet with these beings to prepare a plan for your next earthly life.

In this meeting, you review all of your prior experiences, both on earth and in the spirit world. From this spiritual vantage point, you understand the precise learning that is needed to awaken your divine identity. On first review, you consider the specific divine qualities that have not yet been mastered or need further cultivation: compassion, forgiveness, patience and unconditional love, for example. After choosing one or more qualities to work on, the wise beings assisting you present a variety of circumstances that you could experience in the physical realm to bring each quality into sharp focus. Many choices are available. By accessing the elevated wisdom of your soul (also called the **higher self**, the perfect template of the Divine within each soul), you determine which circumstances will best meet your need to learn that quality.

You next consider which souls from your **soul group** (souls who share a similar spiritual consciousness, most of whom we've had prior experiences with) can best serve all concerned with the intent of spiritual evolution. The karmic ties we have with others will be part of the opportunities set up in the blueprints.

One or more souls volunteer to play the roles that will best suit the needs of the planned lesson. The stage is thus set for the potential future growth of all concerned. The blueprints are then encoded energetically into each soul's memory so that when the timing is correct, in a spiritual sense, the meeting of souls occurs and the planned experience comes about. With these blueprints now encoded, you're nearly ready to be born into a physical body.

What is a Soul Agreement?

It's important to understand that a soul agreement differs radically from our earthly, rational consciousness in two ways:

1. They are unconscious, hidden from our rational mind, and encoded into our soul's consciousness and the subconscious mind. We receive spiritual **wakeup calls**— circumstances, events and relationships that unfold in our lives—to bring these planned experiences to us. Rarely do we recognize these occurrences for what they are when they happen. We're too close to the forest to see the trees, so to speak. That's why trust, faith and perseverance are indispensable qualities to embrace throughout life, especially when events hit us out of the blue.

2. Agreements are just that: they are always in accordance with the free will of souls. If others are involved, the agreement is always a two-way street. Despite what may appear to us as coincidental or random as far as meeting others, our subsequent involvement with them and their impact on our lives (and vice versa), these relationships are actually the result of prior agreements we've made with other souls.

Again, **soul agreements** are always made with the intent of spiritual evolution for all concerned. They are made with unconditional love from a purely spiritual perspective. They answer these questions: *What experiences and relationships, however challenging, offer me opportunities for spiritual growth? Which ones expand the parameters of who I thought I was or could be? What issues come up repeatedly in my life? What experiences and obstacles have challenged the very core of my being? How can I be of service to humanity, animals or the earth using my unique strengths and skills?* To hone in on your personal agreements, I suggest contemplating each of these questions and writing about your observations to gain a clear sense of your unique lessons. Then consider what themes emerge and which ones are emphasized in your life experiences. These are the lessons your soul planned before birth.

Based on my work, I have come to understand that there are two types of agreements that souls make before birth: ones that will involve their own solitary growth through chosen experiences and others that will be shared with one or more souls. These two often overlap since we are all connected on a soul level. Here's how that works:

When meeting with spiritual guides and master teachers before birth, we are fully aware of previous experiences we have had on earth, the lessons we have mastered and the ones that require additional work. Once this is determined, we choose the best circumstances that will bring future lessons to us. Specifically, this includes our choices of birth and/or adoptive parents and their ancestral lineage, our nationality, race, religion (or lack thereof), economic circumstances, physical and mental health (both our own and our parents) and level of intelligence. We also consider inherited physical, mental and emotional predispositions from parents and their genetics, which are contained in the DNA. In addition to genes being physical entities in the body which determine inherited traits, they are also nonphysical *energetic* imprints that likewise contribute to the development of various physical and mental conditions. Energetically speaking, these propensities are karmic threads of thoughts, emotions and beliefs that run through ancestral lines. (For more on how our thoughts affect our biology and bodies, read *You Can Heal Your Life* by Louise Hay [Hay House, Inc., 1984] and *The Biology of Belief* by Bruce H. Lipton, PhD [Hay House, Inc., 2008].)

For example, souls may choose to experience an inherited predisposition to a certain disease in order to master the qualities of faith, trust, resilience, determination, patience, limitation or acceptance that can result from coping with it. Or they may choose a physical disability or illness to become beacons of inspiration for others in their families, the public or organizations dedicated to the same condition.

For sake of clarification about disease and disability, the pre-birth choice to experience these does not mean the person consciously "caused" these conditions; these choices are made through the higher perspective of the soul, not from the rational mind. Several examples of this are children with autism, people with muscular dystrophy, those living with HIV, Parkinson's disease, Alzheimer's disease and other forms of dementia. While individuals with these conditions evolve spiritually for their own growth, they also have the opportunity to positively affect many others, including family, friends, neighbors, communities and the world. In these cases, soul agreements can reach well beyond a soul's individual growth to bring awareness, growth and transformation to others.

In recent times, depression and addiction have been increasingly discussed in the media and on social networks by those who suffer from them and family members who are impacted by them. Despite the obvious tragedy that deaths from suicide and drug overdoses leave in their wake, awareness and discussion of these topics provides hope and education on how to overcome or prevent them. Communication, emotional support and therapy are vital in coping with self-destructive urges for those who suffer from addiction (an epidemic) and crippling depression. In various readings where souls who have passed by suicide or from addiction communicate, they frequently encourage family members and friends to share their stories with others to avert future tragedies. In addition to helping others in similar circumstances, this promotes a sense of purpose and healing to grieving survivors despite the enormous emotional toll these deaths have brought. I discuss more about addiction in Chapter 7.

In the midst of pain and loss, most of us are unable to understand that these life lessons are the very ones we've agreed to learn, nor do we understand how our learning of them impacts others. But when we hurt in the deepest, most raw sense, the opportunity to grow spiritually is the greatest. Let's examine this truth by considering the prior example of Marcia and the loss of her son from addiction.

You will recall that Marcia's father communicated that he and others in his lineage had also suffered from addiction. He came through in the session to assure her that he was looking out for Jason in the spirit world. This message does more than offer comfort to sitters; it also gives powerful validation that those who transition to spirit from previous generations become allies for their families in the physical realm. This is particularly true in cases where unexpected or traumatic deaths occur, leaving unfinished karma from the life just left. I've given numerous readings where older family members come through offering spiritual support for their loved ones. It appears that those in spirit who have had to confront the very same issues express the desire to help others who are stuck in these unhealthy patterns. Older family members are "way showers", so to speak. This collaboration is often an agreement between the two (or more) souls to assist each other in addressing family karma and hopefully bring awareness and healing to the family on earth.

During readings, those in spirit often refer to the repetition of a karmic issue weaving through generations in the family line.

Such was the case with Marcia's family, according to what was revealed by her father. This message served as a reminder about the unhealed addictive pattern that had impacted her family over many generations.

Because we spend many lifetimes with the same group of souls (as well as time together in the spirit world between lives), agreements made between souls ultimately result in the growth of the entire group. What one soul does in any given generation and situation impacts all others in the group. This is why I often tell people that the choices they make in life are capable of healing generations of their ancestral line. It may appear unfathomable to our rational mind but it is nonetheless true, due to the karmic agreements we have with our soul group.

In the event that a person's overly logical mind or religious beliefs don't allow for a medium reading, exchanges between souls can still take place. Spirits can and do communicate to us through inspiration by impressing their thoughts and feelings on our minds, through meditation, answers to prayers, synchronicity, dreams and by connecting us with other people in life. Seeds of healing are planted and cultivated if people are open to receiving them in these ways.

Now let's consider Marcia's soul agreement with Jason, made before his birth. In this case, Jason's soul intuitively knew before birth that he would be confronted with powerful urges to use drugs, based on his family's karmic thread of addiction. He also knew this challenge would affect his family and friends. In a positive sense, spiritual growth for all could result from either resisting those urges—thereby breaking the family pattern of addiction—or by dealing with them successfully through a recovery program. Instead, he chose to allow them to overpower his free will. He became a slave to the addiction, which ultimately took his physical life. It was possible for him to evolve beyond addiction, but not in his current physical life due to his choice to continue using drugs. He would need to start at square one with this same lesson in the spirit world and eventually in his next physical life. In other cases I have seen like this, spirits communicate their regret for the choices they've made, like using dangerous drugs. Once in spirit and after reviewing their own soul's agreement, they realize that they've planned the challenges that overcame them in the end.

Notice that I stated above "others around them" in regards to the spiritual growth of the chosen lesson. In this case, Marcia was an integral part of the plan since (most) mothers are spiritually, psychologically and emotionally affected by what happens with their children. Just like Jason, *she* now had a choice: to continue to suffer, feel guilty and angry, or to move forward and use this tragedy to help her family and others who've faced the same loss. In the process of helping others, Marcia could also bring healing to herself, Jason in spirit and others she would encounter in life. The natural law of karma ensures that what we give to others, we also receive for ourselves.

Marcia stood at a crossroad of choice-making during the time of our reading. Would she remain immersed in pain, anger and guilt, or move forward through the divine quality of forgiveness towards her son and herself? The planned lesson of addiction and its effects had been made between mother and son before his birth. She now needed to decide how best to deal with the turmoil from *his* choice to end his life. In spite of the tragic nature of Jason's death, the opportunity for spiritual growth was still on the table, even though the situation had created considerable suffering for all involved.

This reading illustrates the interconnectedness of souls bound by a soul agreement. One soul's choice (Jason's decision to continue his addiction) lays groundwork for the other's choice (Marcia's option to make the best of a tragedy or continue to suffer) with the opportunity of spiritual evolution for all. As challenging as these lessons are, they often lead to immense growth which couldn't happen any other way.

Pain and Obstacles Motivate Growth

It is difficult to imagine that any soul would volunteer to experience addiction, poverty, war, parental neglect, physical or sexual abuse, mental illness, abandonment or the death of one's child. It's hard to comprehend that we would deliberately choose to experience these harrowing conditions in order to transcend them, thus healing ourselves and others through the pain these circumstances present. Why can't we simply realize that we are divine beings whose essential nature is love? What purposes are served by a body that experiences pain and disease, an **ego** (the personal mind, who you are as a unique being separate from the unity of Spirit) that seems to separate us from others, and emotions that often get the best of us?

The physical world abounds with contrast—good and bad, pleasant and unpleasant. There are ugly, dark, confusing, hate-filled experiences here and also those that are beautiful, kind, nurturing and loving. In terms of spiritual evolution, both are equally necessary. It is this duality that makes earth the perfect schoolroom for souls to learn about their genuine nature of love by allowing them to see who they are *not*. That is the value of contrast as a teaching tool. At times, spiritual growth is frustratingly slow and frequently paradoxical. We must endure suffering in order to transcend it; we must walk a path with pitfalls to see our way clear of it, and we must experience separation to ultimately realize our connection to others and all of life. Only then are we capable of healing ourselves.

Consider this analogy: Would you rather learn to ride a bicycle by reading a book about it or would you choose to learn by directly experiencing what it feels like to ride one? Would it be more helpful to balance your body on the seat, feel your feet on the pedals, gauge the tension of the brakes, coast down hills, or merely read instructions about doing so? Obviously, hands-on experience is more powerful in serving our understanding and mastery of any given lesson. Spiritual matters require the same application of skills. We must go through the necessary "real time" events to gain the wisdom and insight they promise.

Jessica, 38, mother of two autistic children, sits before me in my office. (Prior to the session, she had revealed that she has two physically and mentally challenged children.) A few minutes into the reading, her grandmother in spirit identifies herself by name. "Marilyn" impresses on me that she passed from congestive heart failure. She fills me with feelings of support, understanding and love for her granddaughter. I relay this to Jessica who smiles in appreciation of her grandmother's message. Marilyn had passed into spirit before the grandchildren were born but conveys that she was with these two souls before they were born. Grandma then impresses on me that Jessica is very tired from caring for her children, whom she had vowed to take care of at home after they were born, despite their severe mental and physical challenges.

"Your grandma urges you to take self-care," I tell Jessica. "She says you're very tired and not getting enough rest. You're also highly stressed. She says you thought about hiring someone to help care for the kids but dismissed that thought. Why aren't you listening to her?" I ask.

"I know, I know," Jessica sighs. "Sometimes I feel my gram around me when I'm doing chores. My kids require my personal attention. I'm the only one who can give it. I don't trust anyone else. Their father isn't very involved with them. He works all day, so I'm it as far as caretaking duties. I haven't told anyone this, but sometimes I wonder why this has happened to me," she says with downcast eyes.

I can feel Jessica's exhaustion and resignation. I explain that those in spirit are aware of our life energy by tuning into our thoughts and emotions. They do not want to see us go through unnecessary strife although they cannot interfere with our free will. Jessica's grandmother had obviously been trying to help her understand the need for self-care. Hopefully she would heed this well-intended message to avoid total burnout.

I sense there is something more Marilyn wants to impart to her granddaughter in this communication, a message about the two children. *Yes, there is surely something more here,* my gut tells me. I close my eyes to listen through **clairaudience**.

"She says your two kids are brave souls who have come to help others through their own challenges," I share. "These two are actually advanced souls who've agreed to come to earth and teach others about compassion and overcoming obstacles. She says that both you and your husband are growing spiritually by being their parents, even if you can't see that. They can affect many others by their example and so can you."

Jessica's face lights up. Despite her exhaustion, she manages a smile. "I've always felt that in my heart! In fact, I felt that shortly after each was born. When I look into their faces, I feel God telling me they have a special purpose in life. It gives me hope in the midst of all this tiredness! It's not easy by any means, but hearing this validation from my grandma definitely helps."

After the reading, Jessica tells me that throughout their short lives, her children had encountered many people due to numerous hospital visits and physical therapy sessions, and in weekly visits to the grocery store, church and parks. They had also been featured in a local newspaper and a TV news segment about children with disabilities. I had no doubt that these courageous souls would go on to touch many more people in years to come, thus fulfilling their own soul agreements and, at the same time, inspiring others with similar conditions.

There is another vital lesson that we can take from Jessica's story: It's best to not judge what we don't understand through our limited minds. *That is, we rarely grasp through rational perception alone the real meaning of what is taking place from the soul's elevated perspective.* Unlike the rational mind, the soul knows only the perfection of Spirit within itself and others. That being true, we are fortunate if we come to understand our own lessons, let alone those of others. What appears as a vexing problem from the personality's perspective is actually a valuable asset where the soul is concerned. Thus this paradox of spiritual growth makes sense when it comes to perceived deficits in life: Less (of anything on the physical plane) can mean more (spiritually). Likewise, those who are "last" from the ego's view can be "first" in terms of spiritual understanding. Again, the soul's perspective differs radically from what the rational mind perceives. It is only possible to understand it by accessing the expanded vision of the soul through meditation, prayer and stillness, which I discuss in Part Three.

How can we learn to face, navigate and ultimately grow from what life presents? The key to this is acceptance of the circumstance. That does not mean we are thrilled about coping with a serious illness, going through a bitter divorce or losing our life savings to bankruptcy. Acceptance means we meet life on life's terms without attempting to immediately attack and solve problems. Surrendering in this way lessens resistance in any given moment and helps to alleviate suffering. Surrendering makes us stronger during adversity by building trust and faith in the wisdom and direction of our higher self. From that standpoint, we make choices about how to proceed in the next moment. It means that we recognize the challenge as an opportunity to move beyond the particular limitation it presents. It is our choice to use that opportunity for growth or to remain imprisoned by it.

Spiritual Growth, Karmic Lessons and Reincarnation

Even if we acknowledge that we are eternal beings whose real identity is Spirit, we frequently question the purpose of our lives, especially if we feel unfulfilled. Similarly, we may wonder why we need to experience particularly difficult relationships, unexpected situations and traumatic events. *Why are things going the way they are when I planned otherwise?* we wonder. This conjures up the old adage: "If you want to make God laugh, tell him your plans."

Despite outward appearances, circumstances do not merely "happen" to us; they often contain hidden gems for us to mine if we are willing. In my quest to discover the truth in the early stages of awakening spiritually, I asked my spirit guides many questions: *Why do we take physical form in the first place? Are we to learn specific lessons that we ourselves set up long ago in the spirit world? Is there something at work behind the scenes that is unfolding, something about which we have no clue or any control? How can we find out what this is?*

Over the course of many years and difficult circumstances in my own life, I've gained insight about these and other metaphysical questions through mediumship, intuition and studying the writings of spiritual teachers. Although I do not profess to have concrete answers to these questions that have confounded humanity for thousands of years, I do have direct experiences revealed through my work that shed light on these enigmas. Through the course of thousands of readings, spirit guides (my own and those of sitters) have communicated that we indeed choose life plans before birth to learn vital soul lessons.

The primary lesson about the forgetfulness of our true nature as spiritual beings is common to all souls. Upon incarnating into a physical body, most of us have little (if any) remembrance of the formless, relatively perfect world we came from before birth. That world is our true home since we are first and foremost Spirit. Eventually, we will have no need to return to earth upon completion of all of our lessons; we will be one with Spirit at last. While here in physicality, however, we frequently get lost in the world of contrast and form.

How often do we falsely believe we *are* our bodies or the thoughts of our rational brain? In my observation, these erroneous beliefs are the root cause of anxiety, which is rampant today. We endlessly judge ourselves and others. We carry the expectations of society or think we should be somewhere other than where we presently are. We can successfully free ourselves from the resulting anxiety generated from these depleting beliefs by accepting that they are products of mental conditioning and nothing more. Problems arise when we believe they are true. The spiral of anxiety then begins to build and we become lost in the illusions of our own thinking. In Part Three, I write about the useful tool of mindfulness that will help you to acknowledge these thoughts but not cave under their presence.

Although the concept of **reincarnation**—the soul taking physical form numerous times—may not be accepted by everyone, I have seen firsthand how it is true. When I initially gave readings, I had no intent of receiving prior-life information for sitters. A year or so after I started, I was startled to see scenes and receive impressions about these images over sitters' left shoulders when they sat before me. These scenes were typically from a time period other than the present; the impressions involved specific circumstances, beliefs, feelings and various issues sitters had experienced from that time period. At first, I was confused by these occurrences but soon discovered that when I shared them, sitters resonated with them. Often, the scenarios I saw related to a karmic theme that they immediately recognized as interwoven through their lives. Eventually, I discerned that these themes were repeated in order to be dealt with in souls' physical lives and were all "part of the plan."

In most readings, I've found that people are receptive to hearing this information about their life patterns and chosen soul lessons. They take it as validation of what they previously felt and use it to transform unproductive patterns of behavior. Some, however, are not yet ready to confront these unhealed aspects of their own ego defenses. When this occurs, there is nothing I can do except deliver the information as best I can. Consider this example from an early psychic reading in which the theme of responsibly using one's personal power is highlighted.

Kara, 25 and stunningly beautiful, is seeking guidance about two romantic relationships that she is having simultaneously. Which man should she choose to commit to? She is significantly stressed over this quandary and tells me she wants the answer through our reading.

In advance of the session, as I do with all clients, I advise her to prepare by writing questions and engaging in meditation or stillness. (This preparation is very helpful because it brings clarity and intent to sessions. It is much like making an appointment with the spirit world to communicate.) I also explain that a reading is merely a signpost to help with life direction, and that I can't and won't tell her which man to choose. After hearing this, Kara still insists on having the reading. (Note: No reputable medium would ever profess to have "the answer" to anything. That responsibility belongs to the individual having the reading. All too often, people do not want to assume responsibility for their own choices.)

Shortly after reciting my opening prayer, a clairvoyant image of a Victorian-era parlor with a man kneeling in proposal of marriage to a seated woman appears over Kara's left shoulder. In this scenario, I sense the woman's arrogance and the man's emotional pain as she rejects his offer. Through **claircognizance** (inner knowing), I sense that this man continued to pursue her despite her rejection.

Upon relaying this to Kara and stating its relevance to her current situation, she blushes and admits that she had rebuffed one boyfriend's advances because he did not make enough money according to her standards; however, he persisted in contacting her. The other man she is seeing is, by her own admission, a "nice but boring man." I sense it is because there is no tension or drama in the relationship and to Kara that equates to boredom. She states that she feels "comfortable" and "safe" with him, but for the most part, uninterested; but she is reluctant to let him go because of her fear of being alone.

The past scenario obviously connects with her current quandary. The same theme of arrogance is now playing out in Kara's life. She states that both men refuse to accept that she doesn't care for them and they try even harder to garner her attention (as shallow as it was). I sense that she takes some sort of strange pleasure in throwing them morsels of affection and stringing them along. This gives Kara a false sense of power. She admits that both shower her with praise, treat her to expensive dinners and pamper her with various gifts (which they cannot afford). It quickly becomes clear to me that what she is doing to these men is nothing short of cruel, considering her opinion of them. It's a serious misuse of her personal power, even though they are complicit to this treatment. She is doing it to satisfy her own selfish needs.

I explain to Kara that both relationships are bringing forth a karmic pattern—the correct and wise use of her own power—that she desperately needs to address. If she continues to play this game she would build further karma for herself through this destructive pattern, as well as contribute to others' emotional pain. Upon hearing this, she stands up in an angry huff and moves toward the door, about 15 minutes into the half-hour session. This is obviously not the direction she had hoped the reading would take; she wants "the answer" without any regret or the necessary adjustments in her own psyche to change a long-held pattern. As she exits, I vow to myself to not take her dismissal of the information personally, although I feel tense and upset by her reaction. At the very least, I tell myself, the reading planted a seed of soul awakening within her, though she couldn't (yet) acknowledge it. She simply wasn't ready to receive guidance, but she's young and has a lot of life ahead of her.

Our Shadow Selves

Regarding relationships, we draw people to us who reflect the level of consciousness we emit. In fact, the spiritual value of *any* relationship is to recognize the reflection of ourselves in another, both good and bad qualities. If we are open to allowing it, relationships can reveal hidden aspects of ourselves that need to be brought to light for healing. These are sometimes referred to as **shadow selves**, suppressed thoughts and emotions that we consider unacceptable in ourselves. They are suppressed due to denial, shame or fear on our part. In the reading with Kara, her shadow self was one that sought power over others due to her own perceived lack of power within herself. She also feared being alone. Until she realizes that this is why she feels unfulfilled and unhappy, she will continue to repeat these destructive patterns in relationships.

It's far easier for us to see and react to our own shadow by seeing this same propensity in others' behaviors. We react to these patterns by criticizing or condemning others instead of reflecting upon why we're upset by their words and actions. Pointing the finger at others is much easier than delving into our psyche to discover our own shadows. Spiritual integrity requires that we examine all of our aspects to reveal the light within. Relationships can help in this process by showing us what we need to address and heal in ourselves.

Because we are always emitting life force energy, we draw others to us and vice versa, based on the quality of that energy, regardless of our conscious mind's absence from the process. Some meetings between souls involve the resolution of deeply held "negative" debts such as murder, rape, abuse or theft. As incredible as it may seem, these cases also involve agreements between souls for the purpose of growth. We may spend many lifetimes mastering one quality such as forgiveness, faith, generosity or self-respect. How would it be possible to learn forgiveness if we had no one to forgive? How could we recognize our soul's authentic power if we had not first believed we were a powerless victim? Karma is complex, with much depth and many layers in individuals, between two people and within families. It cannot be simplified or glossed over. The best way to understand our souls' lessons is to approach them with open-mindedness and without judgment of self or others.

Based on what I have seen in my work, the majority of our life experiences are influenced by our subconscious mind, the hidden vault of all of the soul's experiences across the eons. This is also the domain of the lessons we plan before birth. These energetic codes are part of our higher awareness, even though we have no conscious remembrance of them. When our soul's consciousness is ready, they will manifest into physical expression. In the next chapter, you will learn how lessons are encoded within the soul's memory banks, as well as how to recognize them and release those that no longer serve your growth.

Two. Akashic Files: The Soul's Memory Banks

Upon time and space is written the thoughts, the deeds, the activities of an entity—as in relationship to its environs, its hereditary influence; as directed—or judgment drawn by or according to what the entity's ideal is. Hence, as it has been oft called, the record is God's book of remembrance.
~ Edgar Cayce

It's a balmy spring evening at the Open Mind, a metaphysical shop near Pittsburgh. James, a well-groomed man in his late fifties, stands up from the back row during the question segment of the mediumship program I am leading.

"I don't know why I'm here this evening," he begins, his voice quivering. "I saw the sign out front about your program and it drew me to come in. I feel kind of silly asking this, but ..."

James' voice is suddenly drowned out by several large booms coming from the street below the upstairs room where we're gathered. I recall that today the town is celebrating its founding date by holding a street carnival with fireworks. Many in the group look anxiously towards the windows. I remind them about the celebration. Several people chuckle and remark how close the store is to the fireworks' launch point. I focus in again on what James is asking. Although I didn't realize it then, the loud booms heard at the exact moment James began to speak would turn out to be an astonishing synchronicity directly related to his concerns that evening.

"Um, as I was saying," he continues, "I don't know why I came but something told me you might be able to help me with a problem I've been having since I visited Gettysburg [Pennsylvania] Battlefield [from the Civil War] last year. Since that time, I've been haunted by anxiety, losing sleep and feeling restless. I don't know why this is happening. Do you have any insight that could help me?" he asks.

"This is an intriguing question, for certain, but not one that can probably be answered tonight during my program," I begin. I pause to tune into his energy before responding. I sense the insight he needs is not a message from his loved ones in spirit, but rather one from his spirit guides who have knowledge of his Akashic file. I suddenly feel an emotion coming through me, which I relay to James.

"Would you understand feeling guilty for some reason?" I ask him. "I do not know why, but that is the feeling I pick up around your being there at that battlefield." As is usually the case during readings, I have no idea what the message means but trust the impressions I receive.

James nods. "Yeah, there is something going on with that feeling of unexplained guilt! I just can't put my finger on it."

I ask him to see me after the program to further discuss this issue. He agrees and sits down.

After the program concludes, James makes an appointment to come to my office for a past-life regression to hopefully discover the root of his peculiar emotional distress. In my early training at Delphi University, I learned how to conduct these sessions, which involve guiding clients into a light hypnosis to obtain information from their Akashic files. This therapy is based on the premise that current life circumstances, beliefs, attitudes and perceptions frequently stem from prior experiences we have had. Once we see that these no longer serve us, they can be released. Although I no longer conduct regressions, these interactive sessions have proven to be of great value in helping people understand the roots of fear, anxiety, guilt and other emotions. Healing and growth occur more quickly as a result.

Fast forward a month or so: Just prior to the session, James tells me that his feelings of anxiety and guilt were particularly noticeable upon viewing a painting depicting a battle scene on a tour he took of the Civil War battlefield. He reports that since that day last year, he has been troubled by all of the negative feelings, particularly guilt.

During the regression—in a state of light hypnosis—James accesses a former life in which he was a commander in the Union Army during the Civil War. As I sit beside him rapidly taking notes, he relates specific battle maneuvers, names of soldiers and details of what his life was like during those days of war. He shares feelings of overwhelming guilt after one battle ends in which many of his men were injured and killed. Further, he relates that he was accused by those in his unit of making unwise decisions while in command. Even though he did the best he could at the time, unforeseen obstacles caused his defeat in the battle. This blame led to his feeling ashamed and guilty about the deaths of his men who trusted him. The information flows so quickly from him that I can barely keep up in my note taking. After a while, the information slows. I lead James back to present-day awareness through another guided meditation.

After the session, James and I are both astonished by the amount of detail that had come through. Further, all of this appeared to be compellingly relevant to his vexing anxiety and guilt. After the regression, he is drained emotionally but says he feels more at peace than he's felt in months. He has finally made sense of the unexplained, troubling feelings he's had all year. The painting sparked the long-buried remorse from his days during the war, particularly relating to his perceived failure in leadership. Now that he knew the troubling feelings were based in the past and were unfounded to begin with (since he was not directly responsible for these deaths), James could more easily cope with and release them.

During our follow-up discussion, I'm suddenly hit with the memory of the loud booms during the program at the moment James stood up. Could these be reminiscent of the sounds of cannons and gunfire on the Civil War battlefield? *What an astonishing synchronicity!* It seemed incredible but we had both witnessed it and there seemed to be a connection. I felt tingling in my legs, a sign of validation for me.

"The boom of the fireworks during my program ... well, I can't help but think that the universe was giving validation of what you were going to ask. A portal of energy opened that night. That's quite amazing, isn't it?" I ask.

James is silent for a moment. "Yeah, it sure is. I can't get over all of this. I never imagined I would regress to being on a battlefield in those days. I need time to put this all together."

Before James leaves, I advise him to ponder the newly surfaced information, taking note of any nuances in his emotions, thoughts and dreams in the days ahead. I suggested he record them in a journal.

A few weeks later, I receive a phone call from Julie, James' fiancée. She says that she has no idea what we discussed the day of James' session, but he is a much different man after having it. Apparently he didn't share the details of his session with her but soon after, she noticed that he was calmer, happier and more carefree than she had ever seen him. He had also begun sleeping through the night instead of tossing and turning as he had previously.

"I noticed a change with him right after the session," she shares. Before hanging up, Julie thanks me profusely. "The change in James is remarkable! Whatever happened in that session really helped him."

The session apparently cleared the old emotional debris from James' Akashic file, freeing him to live without the encumbrance of the past. Although I do not know if he was able to validate the battlefield information relayed during the regression through research, after hearing from Julie, I have no doubt that James' life took a turn for the better once he obtained conscious knowledge of his previously distressing emotions.

James' extraordinary healing is one I've witnessed in others who undergo regression therapy to get to the root of troubling emotions, relationship challenges, problems with money and illnesses. Not all the experiences we have can be attributed to prior ones, of course, but many do repeat because we attract them based on similar thought forms in our present-day consciousness. Various events, experiences and incidents in our current awareness—such as James' visit to the Gettysburg Battlefield—act as sparks that reignite these previously buried memories that are stored in the files.

When these incidents occur, they can be startling and even frightening since we have no conscious remembrance of them. We may overreact or be emotionally triggered by a seemingly benign event, place or interaction with another person. In some cases, people become inexplicably ill, anxious or depressed. These charged reactions occur due to the similarity of the energy of the current event and the one from the past. They can bring up repressed thoughts and emotions from the subconscious mind. If these types of experiences weigh heavily on you or affect your ability to function normally, I suggest you seek the help of a qualified person who has been trained in past-life regression.

The Soul's Report Card

In some sessions, spirit beings impress on me that after death, they saw their recently departed lives in panoramic vision, including relationships, choices and the impact their lives had on others. As mentioned in the reading with Marcia in Chapter 1, this assessment or life review is a complete record of the soul's consciousness during physical life. In spirit, souls feel what others connected to them felt. They gain knowledge of the underlying implications of their actions, how they affected others and how their lives contributed to the whole of humanity. Importantly, some spirits "grade" themselves on how well or poorly they did in life from a spiritual standpoint—a report card, of sorts. In cases where choices harmed others or were self-defeating, they give insights about what they now understand that they could have done better. These compelling testimonials are enormously valuable to sitters who are open to receiving this soul wisdom. These types of messages help others transform by avoiding the same mistakes. It can also teach surviving family members about previously hidden or unaddressed painful family patterns by bringing them to conscious awareness—the first step in healing them. Consider this example from my case files:

During a reading with Candace, the theme of physical and emotional abandonment arises when her father comes through and reveals that he should not have abandoned her when she was a young child. He left to avoid the responsibility of providing for his family and to pursue his own self-centered interests. At one point during the session, he shows me the clairvoyant symbol mentioned in Chapter 1: a thumb pointing backwards, indicating the same theme has replayed with generational family members. After passing into spirit, he became aware that his choice to leave repeated a pattern set up by his great-grandfather and father. They had both left their families struggling to survive due to their abrupt departure. Because he now sees the hardship his choice created for his own family, he tells Candace that he should have instead chosen to stay with them. After he left the family, he had little communication with her until years later, shortly before his death. During that time, Candace visited him as he was dying from cancer. No words about the past were exchanged between the two before he died a short time later.

At one point in the reading, the man relates that he has seen how his departure affected Candace throughout her life, particularly concerning three traumatic divorces she endured. Spirit impresses on me that all of the men she chose to marry were emotionally distant, uncaring and verbally abusive, much like her dad. Because of her childhood, Candace had a deep fear of being alone; anything was better than dreaded loneliness. Ironically, she chose men who, in one way or another, abandoned her both physically and emotionally—the same behavior her dad had shown.

Near the end of the reading, her dad asks for forgiveness. Upon hearing this, Candace cries. Also revealed in the session were Candace's pre-birth plans with her father, which included the issues of abandonment and self-worth. Her lesson was to learn and evolve from the pain of not having her father in her life, and instead of repeating it in relationships, she could rise above it to discover her self-worth. (I discuss more about abandonment in Chapter 7.)

"For a long time, I thought I was responsible for driving him away," she admits. This irrational belief is common among people who have a parent leave during childhood. Children do not have the capability of adult reasoning and understanding; they believe they have done something wrong that causes a parent to withdraw love and support.

After Candace's session, she tells me that she finally sees why she's had many difficulties in relationships over the years. This was something she hadn't connected with the childhood pain of losing her father.

"I thought I was undeserving of a stable relationship. Now I see that my perceptions were skewed from early on," she says.

As far as grades go, I believe Dad would have given himself an "F" in his duties as father in this case, but in the end, he received some redemption from his prior choice by acknowledging his personal responsibility for making that choice, something he had neglected to do during his physical life. At the same time, he helped to shed light on his daughter's troubles. She had been unconsciously playing out the trauma of her childhood.

"I now know to stop carrying others' problems," Candace shares after the session. "I thought other people could give me happiness but that is up to me. When my dad left years ago, there was nothing I could do. I felt helpless and afraid. Now I know it wasn't my fault. I feel as if I've been reborn today."

Each soul makes the determination of what "grade" it has earned on a given lesson chosen in the pre-birth blueprints. During that process, we are not deceived by our ego defenses because those exist only on the physical plane. The truth is revealed through the omniscience of our soul. It is difficult for our rational minds to grasp the concept that, in spirit, our personality—with its relatively limited perception—is overshadowed by the brilliance and perfection of our soul. I often have to explain this to people who question why particular messages communicated by family members seem completely out of character, based on their previous experiences with them. In spirit, the truth of one's character is made clear and correction of unbalanced karma must be addressed for further spiritual growth. If this fact is not known to sitters, the opportunity for reconciliation between those in spirit and those on earth can be missed. This was highlighted during a group reading I did a few years ago.

"I have Mom coming through for you," I say, pointing to Sara, a middle-aged woman who sits in the third row of the gallery reading. Her face registers surprise when I come to her. She fidgets in her seat, yet I know I have her full attention.

Just then, I sense her mom wants to connect with someone else there besides Sara. "Who did you come with today?" I ask.

"My sister, Dawn," she says, touching the arm of a woman on her right side.

Clairvoyantly, I see the mother standing between her two daughters. "She is here for both of you," I tell them.

Both women sit up straight in their seats and look at me intently.

"Your mother impresses on me that she had lung disease and mentions the name of Helene," I continue.

Sara gasps. "Helene is her name. She had emphysema," Dawn confirms.

"She wants to let you know she's aware now that she was not a good mother to you. She was too selfish, she says. She didn't see that at the time, but now openly acknowledges it and asks for your forgiveness."

Dawn shifts forward in her seat, visibly agitated. Sara's face contorts into a scowl. *Oh-oh,* I think. *This message definitely strikes a nerve.* I pause and wait for either woman's response to this unsettling message.

"Oh, how wonderful," Sara says sarcastically. "Of all things for her to say! She was a narcissist! It was always about *her* needs, even when my sister and I were young kids. You mean to tell me she's sorry now after all these years? Right! I don't believe it!" Sara waves her hands in rejection of the message.

I'm taken aback by Sara's strong retort but continue with the reading. "There's more. Are you open to hearing it?" I ask them.

"Sure, but I don't know that I believe she would admit how terribly she treated us. That's not like her," Dawn remarks.

I know that I'd better explain the workings of the spirit world so Sara and Dawn understand the reason their mother was coming to them in spirit. "She is now aware that she could have done much more for others, specifically her family. She wants you both to know she is working on correcting that in spirit. She will now help you—through inspiration—with whatever you need. She knows she didn't do that while here, so needs to do it now. She asks you both to accept this if you can. She's changed from the person she was while here. This is an opportunity for a three-way healing: for both of you and for her," I finish.

I sense from the stern expression on both women's faces and Sara's crossed arms that they are still not receptive to hearing their mother's message. At this point, I feel the mom's energy connection with me recede. There was nothing more to say. Her reason for coming through was complete, at least from her perspective. She knew she could not force her daughters to accept her newfound awareness. Some spirits are relatively cut and dried in what they want to communicate because they have only a single message to share. I pause before moving on to reach others in the group. I had done my part in delivering the message. It was up to Sara and Dawn to take it or leave it.

One of the toughest lessons I've had to learn as a medium is that I am never responsible for how people react to a message I give or what they do with the information in it. As illustrated in the past-life reading with Kara from Chapter 1, the most challenging part of my work is to witness sitters' rejections of what Spirit imparts to them, although I know that some are simply not ready to move beyond old wounds. We are either ready to hear the truth or we are not. We choose to transcend pain or we are content to stay locked in it. Yet there is no denying that we cannot "un-hear" what we hear. At times, people have thanked me months or years later, saying that they were unable to accept the information at the time of their reading but reconciled it later. In the case of the two sisters, I assume that process may take considerable time, given the deep wounding that both obviously carried.

The Spiritual Purpose of Painful Agreements

As you can see, some souls make blueprints and agreements with other souls that are exceedingly difficult when viewed solely from an earthly perspective; yet they are necessary for the spiritual evolution of all involved. The reading with Sara and Dawn is an example of difficult karmic agreements between family members. Yet how would we grow if not challenged in life? Although this is indeed possible—and hopefully will be what we (as a species) evolve into in the future—most of us gain the most by overcoming obstacles and setbacks. Such is the case with murders, rapes, betrayals, disabling or fatal accidents and other harrowing situations as previously mentioned. Of course, this idea is unfathomable to most people since the rational mind perceives victimhood in these circumstances.

The mind and personality, which function in earthly duality, subscribe to the idea that there are victims and perpetrators. My experience with mediumship has shown otherwise. Although we aren't consciously aware of it, we experience life at the discretion and guidance of our soul. The short example below is one in which a young man who passed from murder imparts a surprising message to his sister about his pre-birth agreement with the people who took his life.

Sharon tells me she sought out a reading with me with the intent of obtaining information about who had taken her brother's life. The family understandably wants justice and they are fiercely bent on identifying and finding the murderers, she informs me. Upon tuning in that day, her brother in spirit gives limited information about the specifics of the murder scene and instead insists that he had already made peace with what had happened to him. He further impresses on me that this is because the murder—an agreement between him and two other souls—was part of his soul's blueprint to address prior karma. As I deliver this message, I'm initially stunned by his seeming lack of concern.

Needless to say, this is a difficult message to give to Sharon but she is surprisingly receptive to it—an indication of her spiritual awareness. Overall, her brother gives me the impression that his death was "no big deal" and that he was doing well in spirit. Clearly, this young man is a spiritually advanced soul.

"I believe that he would have this attitude about his death because my brother wasn't a vengeful person," Sharon comments. "He tried to help others as much as he could. My family may not be open to hearing that message from him, but I am."

This type of message is a hard pill for most people to swallow, yet I know it is true based on the soul's knowledge of pre-birth planning and the resulting evolution of all involved. In this scenario, lessons of cultivating forgiveness for the young man and his family appeared to be a central theme. They could all evolve from his tragic death.

Another example of a challenging blueprint is a debilitating accident that changes the very core of one's life. In these cases, souls have made plans to experience detachment from the physical body (in some cases, from the mind) to evolve. In many instances, they are also instrumental in the evolution of others. Given that most of us identify with our bodies and minds, severe limitation of these allows focus on one's inner identity, the awareness of the soul. This is another instance in which the experience of duality (body versus soul) offers opportunity for growth.

Christopher Reeve, star of the *Superman* movie and its sequels, is a soul whom I believe signed up for this particular lesson. After being paralyzed from the neck down as a result of a horse-riding accident, he was confined to a wheelchair and had to use a respirator. But as the world watched, he not only became an avid supporter of handicapped children, he started the Christopher Reeve Paralysis Foundation, which advocates for research in spinal cord injuries. He also resumed acting and directing films, as well as authoring his autobiography, *Still Me*, an appropriate title. When he passed in 2004, he left the legacy of his selfless work to help others, something that would not have been possible without his incapacitation.

Of course, not all blueprints involve troubling circumstances. On the other end of the spectrum are lives well lived with no regrets. Contained within these messages from the spirit world are validation and confirmation for plans that played out in a positive sense, including adherence to spiritual principles such as service to others.

Recently, I did a phone reading for Susan, who heard from

her brother, Frank, in spirit. At the beginning of the half-hour session, the man identifies himself by promptly impressing me with several facts about himself and his family. He had been a teacher for many years, he says. He mentions the value of education, something his father had stressed to him. Frank then makes reference to Susan's sons (both teachers) and their advanced degrees in education (both are PhDs). He states how proud he is of these nephews and gives knowledge of others in the family, mentioning several by name. Further, he impresses me with a connection someone had to the legal system.

After some confusion about this reference, Susan validates that Frank had volunteered to help with his state's education board, which mandates school curriculum. I sense this contribution had probably been part of his blueprint—specifically, his unique contribution of service. From what I could feel, Frank was very much at peace with his earthly life, a message I pass onto Susan. He encourages her to continue writing the children's book she's working on and passes along well wishes for his brother who is ill. The reading ends with these uplifting messages. What could be more gratifying than knowing a loved one is at peace after a well-lived life?

The Rational Mind, Emotions and Beliefs

The Akashic files contain positive, negative and neutral experiences. This includes the creation of our life experiences caused by our thoughts and actions, our reactions to those experiences, personalities we have taken on through various lifetimes, and our attitudes and emotions. These travel with our soul from lifetime to lifetime as well as in between lives in the spirit world. Each lifetime offers opportunities to balance thoughts, emotions and attitudes that are not in alignment with our divine nature. When our soul is on the physical plane, we have multiple chances to remove the layers of karma that are layered over its light. Additionally, we have the opportunity to create new, positive karma that will support and strengthen the divine expression of our soul.

Plans for life on the physical plane made from our soul's consciousness are vital components of the records because they are created directly from the higher wisdom of soul, not from the mind or personality—although these aspects of self play an equally important, necessary role in the incarnating soul's life. Simply stated, our soul knows the perfect circumstances, events and interactions with other souls that will help it to evolve. Tapping into the valuable wisdom of our own intuition gives insight concerning our life direction, purpose and relationships.

We've all found ourselves at one time or another wrought with fear, frustration, anxiety, grief or anger over unexplained events. These emotional states all stem from thoughts produced by the rational, thinking mind, which is relatively unaware of the magnitude, splendor and resilience of the soul. The mind's function is to think, communicate, problem solve and plan—all attributes that are necessary to our survival. However, when the mind over-performs its function, we can easily become lost within our thoughts. This, in turn, produces anxiety and stress.

Instead of recognizing that thoughts are not necessarily true simply because we think them, we often invest in their absolute validity. For example, if we're worried about passing an exam, our stressful thoughts about this can easily escalate into the belief that we will fail it. This belief causes us to freeze in fear during the exam and we end up failing it, due to our faulty perception. We experience life based on our own perceptions. We may become consumed by thoughts that are circular, repetitive and stress producing, which we take as truth. This "over-thinking" can spiral into unbalanced mental states such as rumination, depression and anxiety.

Personally speaking, it's taken me years to learn that in troubling times, the greatest benefits come by relying on spiritual tools that connect me directly to my soul's higher awareness and outside assistance, if necessary. Even if we enlist the help of others—such as psychotherapists, support groups, family and friends—it is ultimately the connection with our own soul that heals us. This speaks to another paradox about spirituality: To find the way *out* (of difficulty) we must go *in* (to access the soul's awareness). This is where we find the truth of our real identity: beyond the mind and personality. This is where we find "the answer" and, importantly, peace.

Before we are born, all prior lifetimes we've had are erased from our conscious awareness so that we may fully focus on the new incarnation. When we return to the spirit world after death, we are once again aware of the totality of our experiences. We then determine how well we lived out our blueprints and what further work is required to meet our chosen lessons. Some souls choose to continue their earthly work in spirit, as the following illustrates:

Christine's brother, Dan, identifies himself by mentioning that he passed from an unintended overdose of prescription pain pills. He gives details about his life, which Christine validates. Dan then impresses on me that he is with others in the spirit world who had also passed at a younger age.

"He says that he underwent training to become a teacher in spirit," I tell her. "He shows me a clairvoyant image in which he is surrounded by teenagers."

I focus in to see more of this intriguing scene. A few seconds later, I see Dan holding a basketball with a circle of young people around him. I convey this to Christine.

"Yes!" she exclaims. "Dan was a high school teacher and a school basketball coach at the time of his death," Christine confirms. "He loved working with young people," she emphasizes. "No one at the school knew he had a problem with addiction. Our family was shocked by his death since we had no idea about the extent of his problem. He hid it very well at work since he didn't want to risk losing his job. Some kids really looked up to him, especially those on the basketball team. It makes perfect sense that he would show you he's continuing to teach and mentor over there. I've often felt that. It's comforting to know he is still doing what he loved."

The Role of the Personality

In life, it's easy to place a premium value on our own and others' personalities and neglect the quiet wisdom that resides in our souls. As life progresses, especially during difficulties, we always have the choice to turn within. In fact, that is the spiritual value of any challenge in life: the opportunity it gives us to move towards the higher consciousness of our soul.

So this begs the question: If we choose specific blueprints before birth, do we also choose our personality? What role does personality play in regard to our soul's plan and life mission? Over the years, my spirit guides have impressed on me that we do indeed choose a personality, which will work with our soul in the lessons it has chosen. This does not mean the merging between the two will be easy; a chosen lesson may well be to transcend a frustrating aspect of personality to allow the purer expression of the soul. This lesson is one I believe we all sign up for at one time or another. Optimally, the personality is what makes us the unique individual we each are while serving our soul's purpose. At the same time, we must realize that this dimension of self is not the totality of who we are. Many people perceive themselves solely in terms of their personality and others get lost within the dictates of it, unaware that their soul is the real navigator of life direction. In fact, some become so over-identified with personality (both their own and others) that they falsely believe they and others *are* their personalities and not spiritual beings who *have* personalities.

Upon returning to the spirit world after death, we once again become aware of our connection to other souls and the universe. Personality falls away as the soul-self reemerges. (Note: Although the personality dissolves in the spirit world, communicating spirits frequently give evidence of their earthly personalities during sessions. This is possible because of their temporary connection during the session with the physical realm. The personality is "remembered" and referenced as it was in the life just lived.)

Having forgotten this truth as we go about physical life, we need reminders of it. These breakthrough moments, reminders or wakeup calls awaken us to the power and presence of Spirit that resides within us. Although we may not be aware of it initially, these events are capable of liberating us from outworn patterns that no longer serve us in terms of spiritual evolution. After weathering the changes that wakeup calls bring to us, we frequently discover that we have developed a life perspective that is different than before these events occurred. In a spiritual sense, these traumatic events serve us by cracking open the shell of the exterior personality and leading us to the Divine within.

In my earlier books, I wrote extensively about the value of wakeup calls—crises such as physical or mental illnesses, accidents, divorce, death of loved ones and job loss—that can positively serve as "portals" into our higher consciousness. If we allow it, these open us to an expanded awareness of inner strength during tough times. They present us with the opportunity to become aware that we are *not* a personality or body—the temporary aspects of self that are subject to change. At our spiritual core, we find reserves of undiscovered fortitude, determination and perseverance that are much greater than we may have previously imagined. When life presents inevitable changes, we have the option of anchoring ourselves to the unchanging soul within. To be clear, the mind, personality and body are necessary vehicles for our soul's expression on the physical plane. Yet as I've already stated, they are not the totality of who we are by any means. In Part Three, you will learn how your unique personality serves your soul and how to recognize that.

The personality is formed partially from genetics and environment (physical aspects) and partially from karmic energies that we carry from previous physical existences. Our emotions, beliefs and attitudes are products of both. Although we do not consciously recall it, these facets of personality are ones we may have had in previous existences. These are specific tendencies that we are born with. Each life experience offers an opportunity to modulate these in various ways. We take them on again and again because we need either a richer experience with them or we've failed to experience them at all. Or we may need to experience certain emotions, beliefs and attitudes to integrate a particular soul quality into our consciousness. For example, if I make blueprints that call for a deeper experience with empathy or compassion, I would choose in my pre-birth planning a personality that is naturally capable of expressing these qualities. I have seen this to be true in people who are from the soul group of those who bring healing to others in various ways.

On the other hand, I could choose to learn about empathy and compassion by experiencing their opposites. I could choose to take on a personality that will incarnate into a family that shows no understanding or compassion for others and neglects my basic needs when I am a child. Through experiencing the absence of these qualities in others, I am given the opportunity to awaken to their worth in myself and others. The negative situations serve as a magnifying mirror to bring those qualities to our conscious awareness. In this case, suffering from childhood neglect serves as a catalyst of spiritual awakening.

Either scenario above highlights the same qualities I've personally agreed to learn, although the first one, in my experience, is admittedly easier, at least initially. We've all encountered or heard of people who surmount unimaginably adverse obstacles to triumph over them and help others conquer similar circumstances. These are not random occurrences; they are divinely orchestrated lesson plans carried out through the higher wisdom of soul, a "soul curriculum" of sorts.

Your Birth Chart Reveals Personality and Reflects Karma

Astrology is a useful tool that I've studied for many years that gives credence to this concept. Because there is so much to learn about the basics of Western astrology, I mention only a few pertinent facts here. To learn more about the basics of this ancient system, I suggest studying any of the hundreds of books that have been written about the topic. Stephen Arroyo's *Chart Interpretation Handbook: Guidelines for Understanding the Essentials of the Birth Chart* (CRCS Publishing, 2004) is an excellent resource for beginner astrology students. A good online resource for learning the fundamentals of astrology and drawing up your own chart is cafeastrology.com.

By looking at the placement of the planets in our birth chart — their signs and houses — we gain valuable insights about the soul's blueprints, its lessons, personality tendencies and karmic challenges. The birth chart is a map of the soul at the exact moment it entered physical life. To gain insight into specific aspects of our personalities, repeated challenges or problems we regularly encounter in life, it's very helpful to understand the basics of our birth chart, which is calculated on the date, time and place of birth.

Each lifetime is unique — as is each birth chart — yet there are repeated themes that souls carry from lifetime to lifetime until they are successfully integrated into its consciousness. These can be interpreted by studying various markers and relationships between planets in the chart that are strong indicators of "carryovers" from previous incarnations.

Aspects of personality can be seen in the placement of the

inner/personal planets (Sun, Moon, Mercury, Mars and Venus) in the birth chart. A portrait and synthesis of the personality can be gleaned by studying these planets' placements in the signs and houses of the chart. Also important are the relationships that the personal planets form with each other and with the outer/impersonal planets (Jupiter, Saturn, Neptune and Pluto) in the chart. These relationships are called "aspects" in astrological jargon. A strong indicator of personal karma is seen in inner and outer planets that "square" one another, or form a 90-degree angle. Squares indicate where we must employ tremendous focus, energy and determination to work through the tension generated from the inner conflict between the two energies symbolized in the planets. The reward for doing so is the integration of the lesson represented by the two planets that form the square. It may take many lifetimes to successfully work with the karma symbolized by a square aspect in our chart.

The placement of Saturn in the chart, in particular, should be considered when looking into karmic lessons, since it reveals the area of life where we will most likely experience setbacks, frustrations, disappointments and growth points. Saturn is known in Western astrology as the ruler of time. It represents the energy of self-discipline, work and personal responsibility. Saturn is also called the "father of karma" because it symbolizes our ability to accomplish and build (confidence, authority, mastership) in the physical world, thus creating or balancing our personal karma. Working with this energy can feel as if we are "unlucky" or being punished at times, but after applying diligent effort to the lessons Saturn presents to us, we are ultimately rewarded by gaining wisdom and experience through the struggle.

Examples of this are the loss of a job, an extended illness or financial hardship. In any of these instances, it's easy to become discouraged, angry, sad or lose hope. Saturn's lessons teach us to stay the course despite obstacles, have patience, take personal responsibility to make changes, and depend on our inner resources to transcend difficulties. In terms of rewards for these challenges and the inner discipline needed to transcend them, Saturn offers us a newfound confidence and inner authority in the previously challenging circumstances. In essence, we grow up in the areas of life that Saturn instructs.

The Scales of Life

How do we know if we are living true to the divine qualities of our soul or if we are giving too much weight to our ego and personality? Do we allow our own light to shine or do we fear it? Do we embrace the divine principles demonstrated by great masters such as Jesus Christ or The Buddha? What guidance system is available that will help us avoid adding more fear, anger, jealousy and other negative emotions to our files?

A simple visual image that is helpful in understanding how we can gauge our progress is a set of scales (an ancient symbol of cosmic justice in Greek and Egyptian cultures). On one side of the scales are the divine qualities we all inherently possess: love, goodness, purity, forgiveness, strength of character, patience, compassion, nurturing and the awareness of unity with all living beings. These qualities exist within the pure state of our soul. On the other side are aspects of ego: fear, resentment, greed, envy, false pride, hatred, competitiveness, self-centeredness and perceived separation from others. Applying this idea to your own life, consider which side is "heavier." To see this more clearly, you may want to journal about the extent of each of these qualities in your life. Which has more of your daily attention? The expression "Lighten up!" means just that: letting go of the relatively heavy energies of the earthly self.

Interestingly, the ancient Egyptians used the image of the scale to depict the assessment of a soul's purity upon death and its subsequent entry into the afterlife. In *The Egyptian Book of the Dead*, the heart of the deceased was shown being weighed on a golden scale by the god Osiris against the lightness of a white feather, representing truth that belonged to the goddess Ma'at. According to the text, the qualities of goodness, harmony, justice and truth were, by nature, light. If the heart of the deceased had embodied these qualities, the scales would balance; if not, they would be imbalanced by the "sins" of the deceased's heart. In this case, the soul could gain entrance into the higher afterlife by first doing penance. According to their ancient culture, Egyptians believed that the weight of the heart was the primary determining factor in the afterlife judgment. It's an assessment of one's character that we refer to even today. How many times have we heard the comment, "(s)he had a good heart," to summarize a person's defining nature?

The symbol of scales also appears on two cards in the **Tarot** deck, which dates back to the Middle Ages. Originally created as a game, the 78 cards eventually evolved into tools for personal and spiritual insight, guidance and divination. Today there are numerous decks of the Tarot created by various artists. Each card depicts themes, circumstances, events and archetypes (universal symbols) encountered by the soul during its earthly journey. The deck is divided into the minor arcana (practical concerns), major arcana (spiritual matters and archetypes) and court cards (people). There are four suits in the Tarot: the pentacles or discs, the wands or rods, the cups and the swords. Although many decks are artistically beautiful, the particular set of cards I've used for many years is the Rider-Waite deck because its imagery speaks more clearly to me than any other deck.

The Justice card (major arcana 11) features the image of a crowned, robed man holding a sword in one hand and a set of scales in the other. Like all of the major arcana, this card represents archetypal patterns within the human psyche and has both practical and esoteric meanings. Its appearance in a spread can refer to justice being served in an earthly court case, usually in favor of the **querant** (the person having the reading) or it can refer to a karmic issue (cosmic justice) facing the querant. In esoteric terms, the sword represents spiritual truth and natural, universal laws; the scales are symbolic of karma that we must balance through harmonious living. Despite cultural or personal thoughts and beliefs about what is correct, divine justice—as set forth in natural laws—always prevails. In both practical and spiritual matters, the image on the card of the scales being balanced speaks to justice being served.

The six of pentacles from the Tarot deck's minor arcana depicts an upper class, well-dressed man handing gold coins to two beggars in rags who kneel beneath him. He holds a balanced scale in the other hand. The literal meaning of this card is "generosity," but it also symbolizes the karmic scales of divine justice, which are perpetually intact. What we give generously to others returns to us and helps to positively balance the energetic scales in our Akashic file. The number six also reflects this principle of balance (since it can be equally divided by two). It also represents harmony and balance in **numerology**, the study of numbers and their meanings.

You Are Forever Adding to Your Files

Because we are eternal souls, the Akashic files are endless; we are constantly adding new material to our soul's records through thoughts, words and experiences. We're also continually creating and balancing karma from our current life and past ones. This will remain true until we (like the **ascended masters** before us) no longer have to incarnate into physical form as part of our evolution. Much like the Egyptians' philosophy, the weight of a good heart, spiritually aligned thoughts and selfless service are valuable assets during physical life and when we return to the spirit world.

Since the condition of our heart is what matters in spiritual evolution, it makes little difference how long we live in physical years. Depending upon their souls' chosen lessons, children and young adults who've had brief lives could very well have accomplished more spiritual work while on earth than some who live to be 90-plus. I have seen how this is so during readings with parents, such as Jessica's in the earlier example. Regardless of their age or relatively early deaths, these spirits have revealed themselves to be spiritually advanced souls. So as you can see, the amount of time spent in a body does not necessarily correlate to the wisdom of the soul.

I hope this chapter brings clarity to you about the power you possess through responsibly using the gifts of free will and right choice in the creation and positive maintenance of your Akashic files. When faced with difficult decisions, ask: *Which choice nourishes my higher self?* Finding the answer to this requires soul searching and introspection by considering each choice and its impact on your life—particularly its role in your spiritual growth.

Each of us is capable of achieving and producing great things if we are willing to combine the resources of our mind, personality and soul. We will explore how to blend these in the final chapter.

Remember that one day you will return to the spirit world and again examine your files in their entirety. Will you have regrets about missed opportunities to forgive or express love throughout life? Or will you be at peace reflecting on a life well lived? The outcome rests entirely on your choice.

Part Two

The Teachings

Three. There is an Afterlife

To the well-organized mind, death is but the next great adventure.

~ J.K. Rowling, *Harry Potter and the Sorcerer's Stone*

Robert, a soft-spoken, kind man in his late sixties, calls me for a phone reading. Before we begin, he reminds me that I'd read for him several years ago during which he obtained much-needed peace. Robert offers no details of that prior reading but tells me that he needs "another injection" of that same comfort. I seldom recall details of past sessions since the information relayed is not relevant to me as the conduit. To preserve the integrity and freshness of the reading, I never ask sitters who they want to connect with. This ensures a clean slate for new information to come through.

After reciting my opening prayer, I recognize the presence of a young man, around 25 years old, with light brown hair. He impresses me with sensations of pressure and impact in my head and upper chest. He tells me that he passed suddenly and unexpectedly. I relay all of this to Robert, who instantly recognizes the man as his son who died in a car accident. The young man gives me clairvoyant images of a lush garden.

"Your son shows me a lovely garden with large stones having inscriptions on them. I see a cast-iron bench. It feels very peaceful in this place. He also wants me to mention the large, shady tree nearby. Does this make sense to you?"

Robert's voice becomes animated. "Yes! You are describing the garden I created in his memory. It's in my backyard and I sat in it just today!"

"He says he is with you there. He wants you to know he is aware that you think of him in that spot. He draws near when you meditate and pray there. There is a journal or pad you write in sometimes when you are there."

"Yes!" Robert confirms. "How would he know that if he weren't there with me? I can feel him with me each time."

As the reading progresses, the young man impresses on me that he and his dad had enjoyed a close friendship. When I mention this to Robert, he validates that they had been best friends as well as co-workers in the family business. The impressions continue to flow.

"Your son wants you to know he's aware of the recent sale of the business you own."

"Yes, that's true. I sold it about a month ago," Robert replies.

I deliver several other messages which all validate this spirit's detailed memories of his life, family and his continued presence around his dad.

"Your son wants you to know he was with you the other day when you were working on the car in your garage."

"I was doing a repair on my car just this week!" Robert exclaims.

"He shows me that the number 19 is relevant to him," I convey. "Do you understand?"

"That's the day of the month he passed."

As the session draws to a close, the son leaves his dad with the comforting message that he will come for him when it's his time to cross into spirit, whenever that may be. I hear Robert begin to cry on the other end of the phone.

"That's one of the questions I had written for today's session," he says. "I know in my heart that it's true he and I will reconnect after I die. The hardest thing I have ever had to face in life is the loss of my son. I think about it every day. Thank you for the confirmations of everything I felt to be true."

This reading represents thousands I've done in which spirit beings communicate knowledge and details of their family's lives in the physical world. In many cases, this knowledge is about events that have transpired *after* their deaths. When facts like this are presented during sessions, it lends credence to the continuity of consciousness after death. In this instance, Robert's son communicated awareness of his father's frequent visits to the memorial garden, a message that brought Robert comfort. He also mentioned the sale of the family business, which happened well over a year after his passing.

I purposely chose this teaching—the reality of an afterlife—to be first in this book because it is the foundation for understanding the eternal nature of the soul and the realization of the enduring strength of love. Moreover, it gives people the hope, faith, comfort and peace necessary to move beyond grief. Without this fundamental truth, all the other teachings would not make sense. After all, if consciousness does not survive death, it would not be possible to receive communication or knowledge from those in spirit.

Consciousness Never Dies

For those who are on the fence about the validity of spirit communication, I attest that not only have spirit beings given details of circumstances I could never have had knowledge of prior to readings, they've also imparted information about which sitters themselves have no knowledge. What is the origin of this information if it is not communication by those in the spirit world?

In a session I did several years ago for Eleanor, her deceased father gave messages concerning his living brother's health—specifically, that he was suffering from shoulder pain. At the time of the reading, Eleanor admitted to having no knowledge of her uncle's problem since she had not been in touch with him for months. When she returned months later for another session, she confirmed that her uncle had indeed had severe shoulder pain at the time of the reading, even though he had told no one in the family about it.

Another memorable example involving evidence of "present day" information is a session in which the name "Elizabeth" was mentioned by Madelyn's mother in spirit, who also delivered a message about family-owned land that had a connection to coal mining. At the time of the reading, Madelyn had no knowledge of either of these references. I suggested (as I often do in sessions) that she notate these messages to see if they would make sense to her later. A few months elapsed before she called me with validation. After talking to her cousin who had done extensive research on the family's genealogy, she discovered that her family shared a distant relationship with Queen Elizabeth II. As far as she knew, Madelyn's cousin was the only one in the family who knew of this connection, as she had just uncovered it. Further, her cousin informed her that early ancestors had immigrated to America from England and had purchased land, which was later mined for coal.

In addition to providing information and details about their lives and families, spirit beings help us to avoid potential accidents and other mishaps. Although I'm uncertain how they are able to foresee events, my theory is that because they reside in a dimension where thought and energy predominate (as opposed to solid matter), they have knowledge of probable future events, which will likely come into manifestation based on our thoughts. I believe this is so because of the law of karma. In other words, everything that we experience in the physical dimension (effect) is first a thought (cause). At times, this pre-knowledge of future events occurs when I least expect it, as in the following story:

After doing gallery mediumship readings at a large expo in Columbus, Ohio, two young women in their late teens approached me as I prepared for a book signing. Out of nowhere, I was intuitively struck by a message to give them. For the record, I rarely do mini-readings after giving gallery presentations. After that type of intense connection with the spirit world, I need to "close my receptivity" to again become grounded in physical awareness. This process helps me avoid burnout due to always having the "switch" on. But this message for the two women had a feeling of insistency about it and felt important to convey. I pulled the young women aside and spoke quietly to ensure privacy.

"I don't know exactly what this means, but an older lady in spirit who is related to one of you—a grandma, I believe—wants you to be very careful while driving, particularly at railroad crossings," I say.

The women look at me curiously. They draw closer to listen as I continue.

"And she says to not drive while drinking. Please, she says, be very careful." With that, the feelings of urgency to convey this message dissolve.

The women shake their heads in acknowledgment of the message but say nothing in response. They thank me and leave the room. I promptly forget the message as I go about the busy day at the expo.

Two weeks later, I receive a call from a woman who identifies herself as the mother of one of the young women that day who had picked up my business card after my presentation. She states excitedly that she was compelled to call me about the message I had given to her daughter.

"I had to let you know something," she shares. "Several days ago, my daughter was riding in a car with her friends and just after they crossed a railroad intersection, another car came barreling through that intersection and nearly smashed into them. The car seemed to come out of the blue. No one was seriously injured but they were all shaken up from the sudden jarring of the brakes to avoid the crash. I can't believe you gave her that message to be careful at a train intersection!" she exclaims. "How did you know this?"

I nearly dropped the phone. "Um, I don't know how, just that an older lady in spirit came to me and insisted I tell them this. Was anyone in the car drinking?" I ask.

"No, at least not to my knowledge," she responds. "But we don't know if the other driver was. He is being investigated. I just had to let you know the message may have saved their lives. My daughter told me she shared your message about the railroad tracks with her friends and warned the driver that day to be careful at intersections and railroad crossings. Well, if they had not been on alert because of your message, it could have been very bad. Thank you."

I hang up the phone. My hands are trembling. The confirmation of the message stuns me even after years of working with the spirit world. I do not understand how the grandmother knew about this future incident but I am awed, humbled and grateful to be a conduit in cases where potential trauma is avoided and lives are saved.

Guidance From Beyond

Another facet of consciousness survival beyond physical death involves messages that give guidance to sitters about their current life challenges—both personal issues and those affecting their families. Although spirit beings cannot change the lessons we chose to learn, they give reassurance about the struggles we are going through. They can inspire and comfort us during the process. We know we are not alone.

Marta discovered this when she called me for a phone session. During the reading, her mother steps forward in spirit and says that she suffered from mental incapacitation before she passed. I hear her give the name "Barbara."

"Mom had dementia at the end. It was hard for all of us since she no longer recognized us when we visited her in the care home. Barbara is my aunt, Mom's sister," Marta confirms. "I wonder what Mom has to say about her."

I silently ask the spirit woman to tell me about her sister.

(These "spiritual interviews" are comparable to those given in person with the intent to obtain information.) In response, Marta's mom impresses me with feelings of agitation around Marta and Barbara's relationship. Something feels off about it. Next, I hear through clairaudience the words "property and money." *Now what could this mean?* I mention these words to Marta in hopes that they will strike a chord.

"Yes! I'm having a very difficult time with my aunt, who Mom put in charge of her estate. We're barely speaking now. You see, I know Mom wanted my son and me to remain living in her house after she passed. But my aunt has been stubbornly refusing and telling us we will need to move," Marta explains in a strained voice. "My aunt also tells me Mom left the distribution of her estate up to her. I discovered through other family members that she manipulated Mom when she was sick. I had no idea at that time. I doubt my son and I will receive anything from the estate now. I've had to hire an attorney to help."

I listen to hear the next impression. "Your mom tells you to not panic about this situation. It will work out even if you can't see it now. Have trust, she says. The situation will improve. She's aware of what's going on."

At this point, I sense Marta's mood shift on the other end of the phone. She seems calmer and comforted by this message. It's confirmation that her mom had knowledge of the family dynamic that she had been struggling with. She wasn't going through it alone. This peace is worth its weight in gold, despite the outcome of the situation (which is still ongoing at the time of this writing).

If I've said the following words once to sitters, I've said them hundreds of times: "Those in spirit know our thoughts and feelings." This rules out mind reading on my part since in many of the sessions, sitters have no knowledge of messages at the time of the reading, but later confirm them. The truth is that spirit beings are aware and alive in a world that is every bit as real as the physical one. Their connection with us is through the indestructible bond of love, which survives death. This is the foundation upon which all mediumship rests in terms of its ability to help people heal.

Arthur Findlay, one of Spiritualism's most esteemed writers, wrote about his experiences with direct voice medium John C. Sloan in the classic book, *On the Edge of the Etheric* (Bristol, UK: WBC Print Ltd., 1986 ed., first published in 1931). Initially skeptical about the validity of spirit communication, Findlay approached the subject by taking on the role of an investigative reporter. He relates multiple experiences as one of Sloan's sitters during séances given by the medium. Direct voice mediums go into trance and deliver messages from sitters' loved ones in spirit through a voice box created from an etheric substance called ectoplasm, which emanates from the medium's body. This type of mediumship is rarely practiced today since it requires exquisite sensitivity, years of development and absolute trust of the spirit world on the part of the medium. It can also be dangerous to the medium's health because of the depletion of vital life energy required to produce the ectoplasm. At the time of my training at Delphi, the school worked with only one person per year in preparation to do direct voice mediumship.

The voices that sitters heard during the Sloan sessions were relayed in the familiar voices of their loved ones and revealed specific, private information of which the medium had no knowledge. Although modern science still does not fully understand how such phenomena occurs, the compelling evidence channeled by Sloan—an ordinary man who lived a simple life—was accurate and impressive. Findlay took every possible measure to ensure the accuracy of the notes he took during the sessions he attended. He interviewed sitters afterwards about any prior public disclosure concerning the messages given. For example, was a fact brought through in the session published in a newspaper or public documents? In no case did he uncover anything questionable; the messages given through Sloan were pure. Many were comprised of information outside of his own range of knowledge; for example, messages given in foreign languages.

In the readings, spirit beings gave facts at the séance about their lives and mentioned circumstances that were known only to their relatives. Some also imparted information about the nature of the afterlife, saying that it was every bit as real as the physical world, although different in its vibration. (The earth plane is relatively dense compared to the spirit world.) Findlay's investigative work lends substantial credence to the existence of a realm in which souls continue to be consciously aware and remain connected to their earth families.

Shortly after his death in 1964, Findlay's wish to start a college for psychical studies was fulfilled with the founding of the Arthur Findlay School at Stansted Hall in Essex, England. Today, the school is internationally renowned and highly respected for its mediumship training programs.

I consider myself blessed to obtain glimpses into the spirit world through my work. Over the years, my spirit guides have taught me about the nature of life in the nonphysical world. If you would like to know more, I share detailed information about the afterlife in my prior books.

Help for Troubled Souls

Perhaps the most startling information I've received during readings concerns messages that also answer my personal questions about the afterlife. For instance, I have always wondered what happens to those who choose to end their own lives. While most people want to know that their loved ones continue on after departing life and are safe and happy, this is particularly true in the cases of suicide for several reasons: Some religious teachings assert that suicide is a sin and those who commit it are drifting (at least for a time) in an in-between state of consciousness — or worse, have been condemned to hell. Those who adhere to these beliefs may have confusion and doubt about the peace and happiness of their loved ones who chose to end their lives. A loved one's sudden and unexpected death is difficult enough to handle without the added trauma of suicide. People who choose this exit strategy are often emotionally and mentally troubled long before doing so. This fact may haunt family members and friends for years in the form of unresolved guilt ("I should have done more to help her."), feelings of helplessness ("I tried to help him but he stopped speaking to me before he died."), anger ("Why did he have to cause us so much heartache?") and grief ("I miss her so much. I'm consumed by sadness.").

In readings where these souls come through, the clear message they typically deliver is that suicide, in retrospect, is not a wise choice. Because the soul lives on, unresolved issues and problems before physical death must be dealt with in the afterlife. There is no escaping one's soul lessons. Add to this the unfinished emotional business with family left behind. Ending one's life adds layers of newly created karma that (s)he must subsequently balance. In essence, suicide creates a loop of energy in which prior lessons, along with new karma, must be dealt with by those who make that choice. Once these troubled souls pass, they become aware that they have created additional layers of unfinished karmic residue that they must now balance.

In some cases, these spirit beings communicate that they undergo counseling in the afterlife, just as we would here. From what I have gleaned, this involves a review of the issues that overwhelmed them — some of which were pieces of their incarnating blueprint. Choices that they've made during physical life are also considered and they are given insights to determine how they veered from their originally intended paths. They continue to work on these karmic issues in spirit.

Personally, I have found that souls who die by suicide are

hesitant when it comes to communication. Some have impressed upon me that they don't want to re-experience the pain they departed with through reconnecting with physical consciousness. It's important to remember that our power of choice in the form of free will exists at all times—here on earth and in the spirit world. This is one of the reasons why a reputable medium can never guarantee communication with a soul during sessions. Each soul must make the choice to communicate, or not. At times, I've had to explain this to sitters who are disappointed when a particular loved one does not come through. It is similar to forcing someone to call, e-mail or text you. It simply cannot be done since we are not in control of another's thoughts or behaviors.

Until a soul expresses the desire to face and move beyond the ego-based thoughts and emotions of its chosen personality, its consciousness will remain limited within those confines— whether on earth or in the afterlife. Most of us are familiar with the daunting task of breaking free from self-defeating patterns and the resulting frustration and desperation when we feel trapped and subdued by them. It requires rising above these thoughts by turning inward to the wisdom and authority of our own soul. This truth also applies in the afterlife, where help and healing are always available. Because of the eternal nature of the soul, a lifetime is like one grain of sand on a beach. Even if this metaphor is difficult to accept in the midst of deep grief, it is nonetheless true. An experience does not define, diminish or destroy the core essence of our divine identity, as harrowing as it may be. It is but one of countless experiences we have as eternal souls.

If you have lost a loved one through suicide, I hope that what I have shared here brings comfort to heal your heart. Although you will probably never be the same as before your loss, please know that your loved one is not "gone" or doomed to damnation. The truth is that no soul ever perishes in the inextinguishable love of

Spirit, but instead receives help and healing in the afterlife.

Knowing We Survive Death Alleviates Fear

Most humans fear the unknown. Even if we are comfortable and flexible regarding change, most of us choose the known, familiar pathway and resist the unknown. I believe this is the reason why many people fear death. When we incarnate, the memory of our true home — the spirit world — is largely forgotten as we mature. This occurs because our consciousness becomes focused on the world of form, the physical realm. In my experience, children are aware of the spirit world until the age of six, around the time they enter school where the rational mind is developed. Some people retain vague memories of what it is like to live in the serenity, harmony and unity of that world, but these fade as physical life intervenes. We have personalities, rational brains and bodies that consume much of our attention. We frequently see others and ourselves as merely one-dimensional (physical).

All too often, the underlying connection that we share with all living beings is superseded by our singular perceptions of aloneness, separation and differentness. It's easier to forget about the reality of an afterlife if you over-identify with the rational mind, the personality or the body. The spirit teaching that there is an afterlife reminds us of the truth of our identity: we are spiritual beings who never truly cease. We return home after our lessons in our physical incarnation are complete.

Among the thousands of readings I've done, some communicating spirits not only affirm their continued existence after death, they also speak of how their former beliefs about the existence of an afterlife were inaccurate. Such was the case with Anna, who heard from her late husband, Gary.

Several minutes into my session with Anna, Gary appears and impresses on me that he was exceedingly logical and intelligent.

Through clairvoyance, he shows me a large stack of books, a symbol that Anna validates by saying he was a voracious reader. In fact, he took great pride in his intellect and all of the book-based studying he did throughout his life. Interestingly, I sense his close-mindedness regarding spirituality even as he connects to me. I pass this feeling along to Anna.

"This makes sense," she confirms. "Gary was an atheist."

Over the years, they'd had in-depth discussions about this topic. Gary was very logical, believing in nothing that couldn't be proven by science. After a moment or so, the reading takes an unexpected turn. I tune in to hear the next message more clearly. *Did I hear this correctly?* I wonder. It doesn't seem to make sense, given Gary's former character.

"He says he wants to tell you he was wrong. He emphatically states that there is an afterlife," I inform Anna. "He mentions that when you two discussed this, you disagreed with him and tried to tell him otherwise. This caused the two of you to argue. Now he wants you to know you were right."

Anna is taken aback by this message. After a moment or two, she responds.

"We did argue about it, that's correct. It's good to know he now realizes there is an afterlife! He and I didn't agree on that topic, ever. We spoke about it shortly before he died, while he was sick. I wanted to comfort him by telling him he will go on after leaving his body. He thought I was silly for believing that."

Another example on that same theme has been given during readings where spirits who've passed unexpectedly—by accidents, murders and overdoses—relate their surprise when they've viewed their bodies from above, shortly after death. These souls describe floating above their bodies, being aware of events and conditions around them and seeing a massive tunnel of light. Because they did not anticipate or intend to die, these spirits are confused as to why they suddenly find themselves outside of their bodies. This seems to be especially true if they had no spiritual beliefs or didn't contemplate the topic of death. Some have said that they stayed at the scene of their death and watched as resuscitation attempts were made. This evidence has been substantiated by sitters when they validate the circumstances surrounding their loved ones' deaths.

After giving readings such as these, I can only imagine the amazement of newly crossed spirits who've had no belief in the continuation of consciousness beyond physical death. Perhaps they know that the messages they give during readings will provide proof of the afterlife and instill peace about their loved ones' future deaths.

Knowledge of a spirit world provides relief to people who feel disconnected from deceased loved ones—one of the most common feelings after losing someone. In other words, accepting that consciousness survives death and that loved ones maintain their connection to us dispels the illusion of separation. People have asked me, "Where is the spirit world located?" My response is always, "Right here." It is energy and consciousness, not a physical location. It's all around us but vibrating at a much higher frequency than the physical world. To perceive it, we must tune into that frequency by raising our own consciousness through the development of our intuitive senses. Knowing and trusting that the spirit world envelops and permeates the physical world also alleviates fear of separation because it is then no longer thought of as being somewhere "out there."

My Evolving View of Death

Although I rarely discuss it publicly, my own view of death has been positively transformed in many ways due to my work in mediumship. Years ago, I feared death because I had no spiritual understanding of what happened after we left the physical world. It's unimaginable to me now that I felt that way, but the fear was very real to me then.

When I was 10 years old, my mom's father passed away after suffering a stroke. He was my first grandparent to die; I had never experienced going to a funeral home to view a body. During the visiting hours, I was afraid to look at my grandpa's body in the casket. When I dared to steal a sideways glance at it, I was shocked by the plastic, artificial look of his formerly familiar "alive" body, especially his hands. They resembled those of a mannequin. The skin covering them was not at all like that of the grandpa I had known; it was exceptionally pale, thin and unnatural looking. As a child, the sight repulsed and terrified me.

That night, alone in my bedroom, each time I attempted to close my eyes, the image of those hands permeated my inner vision. I finally fell asleep but eventually awoke sweaty and restless from subconsciously trying to erase that startling memory. At that age, I did not have the spiritual knowledge that my grandfather's body was simply a vehicle for his soul, which lived on. I also wondered where he had gone. *Was he watching over me now?* That first experience of losing him and seeing his body haunted me like a late-night horror film.

The death of someone close to me did not get any easier a decade later when my Grandma Obley passed away during my second year in college, long before I became a medium. I loved my grandmother and she loved me. I had no doubt about that. She always referred to me as her "dear little granddaughter." I dreaded going to the funeral home. When I attended her viewing, not much had changed from earlier years as far as my perception of death. I was older but death remained an alien and startling "thing" that I wanted to deny as much as possible. Before closing the casket on the day of Grandma's funeral, my grandfather (who survived her) bent over and kissed her face. Standing behind him, I marveled at his forthright courageousness in doing that. As I sheepishly stood by, my mom placed her hand on top of Grandma's in the casket, a simple gesture of affection and farewell. Mom turned around and looked at me in hopes that I would follow suit. I immediately drew back in fear, which was obvious.

"Come on, now. You don't have to do that," she whispered as she took my arm to walk to the chapel for the memorial service.

In that moment, I felt intense guilt and shame for turning away. In my estimation, my unwillingness to touch my grandmother was an abysmal failure on my behalf, given the immense love I had for her. I simply couldn't bring myself to touch her body, as if death were a contagious virus I might catch. That night, again, the nightmares haunted me. Images of Grandma in the casket woke me multiple times. Fear had a paralyzing grip on me because I lacked awareness of the spirit world and had no concept that death was a natural transition in the life of the soul.

My perspective of death has changed radically since then, for which I am deeply grateful. Years of giving readings, studying metaphysics and meditating have transformed fear into understanding and acceptance. I now *know* there is an afterlife and it is nothing to fear. I also know that death is a natural transition that is part of our soul's cycle. I hope you, too, understand this truth about your soul's immortal consciousness.

All Living Beings Are Spirit

A spark of Spirit resides in all sentient beings, including the plant, animal and mineral kingdoms, although the physical forms differ. Some years ago, I intuitively realized that animals have souls that return to the spirit world just as we do. This gut realization was substantiated by several books that I've read about animal communication, as well as my direct experiences of deceased pets' presence in readings. This recognition led me to become a vegetarian five years ago. All living beings are deserving of life, peace, compassion, kindness and respect — qualities that are almost nonexistent in today's profit-driven agricultural industry. After viewing undercover videos of the abuse and torment that is routinely inflicted on factory-farmed animals, I was compelled to immediately change my diet. I did not want to contribute to that cruelty. I also discovered that factory farming causes major pollution to our planet. As I write this, it is my sincere, heartfelt prayer that humans awaken and realize that we are one with all other beings and should act as good stewards in their protection. As divine beings, we owe it to ourselves and all sentient beings to eliminate unnecessary suffering wherever it may be occurring. Expressing compassion for all living beings elevates our collective spiritual consciousness.

Our pets are animals that are particularly near and dear to our hearts. In multiple readings, sitters' beloved pets have come through to communicate their continued connection with their former guardians. In some readings, they appear alone or with other family pets in spirit. At other times, they accompany family members in spirit who say they are taking care of them. An interesting facet of these communications is that animals typically use clairvoyance to communicate their presence. I believe this is due to the fact that they do not have verbal language but instead think primarily in pictures. Various studies into animal psychology and animal spirit communication back this up.

Because I am an avid lover of all animals, it brings me joy to be the conduit for these reunions between pets and humans. Sometimes, I can't help but tear up when a sitter's cherished pet appears. Just like relationships between humans, an indestructible bond of love connects us with our pets. The following reading makes this clear.

Margaret, 65 and a widow, sits with me. After identifying himself by saying he passed from congestive heart failure, her husband, John, shows me a small, lively white dog with him. In my mind's eye, I perceive the dog scurrying around and jumping up and down. I focus in to see if I can determine other characteristics of the dog.

"It looks like a poodle," I say to Margaret. "She has curly, wiry hair and is very animated. She has a little shirt on. Does that make sense to you?"

Margaret puts her hands to her face and gasps. "Yes! That's our dog Fluffy! She lived to be 17. She was like a child to us and I often put little shirts on her. Oh my gosh! I'm relieved to know she is with John. I loved her dearly!"

Next, Fluffy shows me through clairvoyance that she suffered from severe arthritis in her back haunches during later years. I see her dragging her back legs to get around. I relay this image to Margaret.

"Yes, we had to carry her outside to go to the toilet. I felt so badly knowing she hurt. You said you saw her jumping up and down though. What does that mean?"

"It means she is now in a perfect spirit body that has no pain. John is taking care of her. They are together again. That seems to be important for both of them to tell you," I say before acknowledging other spirit loved ones from Margaret's family. Afterwards, she remarks that the message about Fluffy being taken care of by her late husband was the best of all the messages given. She left my office that day beaming.

In numerous readings, various species of pets have appeared to let their loved ones in the physical world know they go on in spirit. I have acknowledged the presence of not only dogs and cats but turtles, birds and horses. Much like human souls, they appear young, vibrant and renewed, free of any physical ailments they might have had on earth. Some have shown favorite locations in and around sitters' homes where they still visit in their spirit form: the kitchen, back porch or yard, for example. Many have shown themselves resting in their favorite spots on the bed or couch. Some are seen frolicking in green meadows and forests in the afterlife.

When we go back to the spirit world, we will meet again with our pets, if we choose. They, like our human loved ones, come to greet us upon our arrival. A popular poem, *The Rainbow Bridge* (original author unverified but widely attributed to William N. Britton), captures the joy of this reunion. It is of great comfort to know that we will see our beloved pets again. Just as with human loved ones, the bond with our pets remains intact, despite death.

Service and Love Go With Us

We come into the physical world as souls encased in bodies until we release those bodies to return home again upon death. Spirit beings in readings frequently stress that the service and love they gave and received while here is what they returned home with. In fact, this is a lesson unto itself: all we take upon our departure are those two intangibles. Nothing else is as valuable in the eyes of the soul. I've lost count of how many times this simple yet powerful and meaningful message has come through. This lesson transcends economic status, nationality, religion, personality and earthly reputation. I believe this is what Jesus meant in His encounter with a rich ruler who refused to give up his fortune to follow Him. He said, "Many who are first will be last, and many who are last will be first" [Matthew 19:30]. When the disciples asked what reward their personal sacrifices would earn them, He replied that they would receive eternal life, not earthly riches. To paraphrase, we earn our place in the spirit world based upon what we *do* while here and not what we *have*. We come into life with no possessions and we leave the same way.

In between birth and death, it's all too easy to get lost in the trappings of material possessions, money, personality and the desires of the ego. In spirit, these earthly priorities are relatively meaningless compared to the majesty and perfection of the soul. The language of the soul—expressed in service and love—speaks softly yet powerfully to us through intuition, relationships, circumstances and life events. What we do and give while here determines our soul's next phase of growth in the afterlife, which is based on the level of consciousness we have upon arrival there. During times when we feel lost, confused or indecisive, we need ask only one question: Which choice, relationship, situation or scenario leads me closer to realizing my soul's divine identity? Listen closely to your heart for the answer and surrender to it with trust.

Four. The Bond of Love is Eternal

Love is the voice under all silences, the hope which has no opposite in fear; the strength so strong mere force is feebleness: the truth more first than sun, more last than star.
~ e.e. cummings

"Your father is here for you," I say to Ellen, 60, during our session. "He says he's been with you in spirit despite his sudden passing from a cardiac issue years ago. He wants you to know he's aware of your accomplishments over the years. He also strongly impresses on me that you have a son and daughter. That seems to be important for him to tell you for some reason. Do you understand?"

Ellen leans forward, enthusiastically responding, "Yes! My dad passed when I was only two years old. My mom has told me stories about him and shared memories with me, but I always questioned if he was aware of me on many occasions. Over the years, I've wondered if he knew about my life as a nurse practitioner and especially about my kids. I don't remember him at all since I was just a toddler."

"Both of your children have done really well in school, he tells me. In fact, he shows me that they have advanced university degrees."

Ellen pulls a tissue from her purse and dabs her eyes. "Yeah, they make me proud. It's good to know Dad sees them. He never knew them, of course."

"Perhaps not in the physical world, but he knew them in spirit before they were born," I explain. "The important message he gives you and his reason for coming through today is that he has *never* left you. He died unexpectedly but he didn't disconnect from you or your family. He's still your dad. No matter what else he communicates today, please leave this session knowing the bond of love between you two is still very much alive."

As the reading progresses, Ellen's father gives details about his life as a police officer. Other relatives in spirit also come through by name and by impressing me with their personalities. Before leaving my office, Ellen turns to me and says, "You have no idea how much it means to me to hear from my dad. I've always wondered if he was watching over me and my family. Now I know."

Of all the messages those in spirit deliver, I believe the assurance that love does not end with death is the most comforting. This simple message appears to touch people's hearts more deeply than any other. When I think back over all the sessions I've given, this message of truth stands tall above all others. Although the manner in which spirit beings communicate it varies from reading to reading, the teaching is the same: The bond of love endures beyond death.

In my observation, this reassurance is why most people seek mediumship in the first place. At its best, it offers hope, peace and healing to those in the physical world from those in spirit. If we know that our relationship with loved ones continues after their departure, we can more easily cope with mourning their physical loss. The realization that we are forever connected to those we love strengthens the bond we share and helps to alleviate the pain of grief. This is not to say that we don't miss their physical presence. We can no longer hold their hand, look into their eyes or embrace them. Nor can we pick up the phone and speak with them. These losses must be acknowledged and accepted in the process of grieving. Yet we can open our hearts to understand that although the physical part of the relationship has concluded, the spiritual, non-physical relationship we've shared continues. Sometimes it is more powerful than we can imagine. I say this based on stories I've heard from clients who have experienced profound afterlife connections without the help of a medium. These connections are generally called after-death communication, or ADCs. I've written extensively about the various types of ADCs in my book, *I'm Still With You: True Stories of Healing Grief Through Spirit Communication.*

On occasions when people contact me to schedule readings shortly after a loved one has passed (if they share that information), I advise them to go through the grieving process first. Because I honor ethics in my practice of mediumship, I consider it my responsibility to tell people that the reading will be of little value if they are distraught through most of it. Although it's understandable that reuniting with loved ones during a reading can be highly emotional, dense emotions such as deep grief must be acknowledged and worked through first to initiate and sustain a fluid connection with the spirit world. Most people appreciate my honesty and call me at a later time when they feel more balanced.

There are no shortcuts and no one-size-fits-all process of grieving. Because of the myriad books, TV programs, blogs and social media discussions about grief, most people today are aware that it should be approached in a way that is personally effective for them. Some people choose to cope with their feelings by becoming introspective and spiritually centered; others obtain relief from talking about their loss to family, friends or therapists. Some prefer to engage in tasks, projects or work to keep busy. Others combine all of these to move on. No one way suits everyone. The focus of healing is to move forward and not remain a prisoner of grief, however that may be accomplished.

The Physical Realm is Temporary

A fundamental teaching of Buddhism is the impermanence of the material world. No living being's body will exist forever; everything (with few exceptions) changes form. This universal truth regarding transformation is set forth in the natural law that states that nothing in the universe is static; everything is in perpetual motion. This constant change is necessary for our evolution.

At mind-body-spirit expos I've attended, Buddhist monks give presentations where they create intricate sand mandalas only to destroy them shortly after their completion. This form of meditation symbolizes the transitory nature of the physical realm. When I initially witnessed one of these demonstrations, I was awed by the depth of emotional detachment that must be required to destroy a beautiful piece of art that took days—in some cases, weeks—to design. Then I realized that detachment *is* the point. The monks consider their artwork to be impermanent, despite the significant time, effort and skill needed to create it.

I've discovered that the need to detach brought to mind another core Buddhist principle: Attachment (to anyone or anything) causes suffering, whatever form that suffering may take. The monks' mandala meditation illustrates the concept of letting go, something most humans consistently find challenging. Releasing attachment to people, places and things frees us from the emotional pain created by clinging to the way we think life *should* be. It opens the gateway to acceptance, a necessary step in healing.

Most of us find it exceedingly difficult to shift our minds away from the perceived need to hold onto someone or something. In my opinion, our rational mind's insistence on holding onto its own manufactured reality—coupled with expectations about the way a situation "should" be—are the root causes of all unpleasant emotions and anxiety. Spiritual tools such as meditation, breath awareness, yoga and mindfulness are effective in soothing these tenacious qualities of mind and leading us into present-time awareness where acceptance lives.

You might ask what all of this has to do with knowing that love is eternal. The answer lies in the truth of our real identity as souls created by the inextinguishable love of Spirit. As I've been sharing, death of the physical body is but one phase of the soul's continuing journey. The essential identity of each soul remains intact and untarnished after releasing the body.

As we are aware, the physical body eventually wears out, breaks down and expires. After the soul's purpose in the physical world is fulfilled, it returns to its home in the spirit world until it is once again reborn into a body. This, of course, is the concept of reincarnation. According to Buddhism and Hinduism, it is the natural cycle of life for all souls, until they are permanently merged with Spirit and do not have to return to the schoolroom of earth. My direct experience with Akashic file readings for people supports this idea of the cyclical nature of life. I do not *believe* in reincarnation; I *know* it because I've personally seen evidence of it. Each lifetime, as well as in-between lives, serves the spiritual evolution of souls. Each lifetime affords the opportunity for souls to express Spirit in physical form. Whether we are here for two, 22 or 102 years, we are given the gift of our personal will to embrace the divine principles of love, kindness, compassion and service, which are expressions of higher consciousness.

What does *not* wear out, break down or expire is the essence of Spirit within every living being. Each soul survives through eternity because it is comprised of the endless energy of Spirit. It is a perfect template of that ever-present energy and forever alive because of that inexhaustible, universal source. As such, it cannot ever be destroyed. It simply changes form. This conservation of mass-energy is a universal law of physics that has become well established since Einstein asserted his famous $E = MC^2$ equation in the early part of the 20th Century. Physicists today continue to decipher the nature of matter and energy as science and spirituality merge.

As human beings with minds that routinely perceive separation and differences between ourselves and others, we need regular reminders that underneath these mind-generated illusions, the bonds of love and Spirit connect us with everyone and everything. Knowing that truth in our heart leads to freedom from every conceivable defense our mind might manufacture against it. In addition, if we know that our true nature as a divine soul is love, we can call upon that power whenever we are tempted to give into fear or judgment. Love is the great unifying force that underlies all of creation.

Mediumship is only possible because of the durability of love between souls in the material and spiritual worlds. Without it, there would be no lasting bond between families, friends and pets. It is the primary reason why people seek continued connection with those they have loved on earth. Love is the healing energy that transcends grief, fear, anger and other lower emotions.

Many metaphysical-spiritual writings assert that love is the glue that unites everyone and everything. Christianity tells us that we are made from the perfect love of God and in His likeness, thus imbuing us with divine qualities. Of course, I am not referring to romantic love here (although that is also an expression of love) but rather the elevated, enduring love of Spirit that flows through all of creation. The Greek term for the love Spirit has for every living being is *agape*, which also includes the love humans have for Spirit. This energy exists in every atom throughout the universe.

The love between souls in its highest form is a direct reflection and expression of Spirit's love. If it's true that energy cannot be destroyed and love is energy, then it is also true that love cannot be destroyed under any circumstances. It lives forever as long as the universe exists. This indestructible quality of love is what the Christian apostle Paul referred to in 1 Corinthians 13:7 when he wrote, "[Love] bears all things, believes all things, hopes all things, endures all things."

Love Never Ceases

Throughout the years, I have given many group readings to a variety of people from all walks of life. At the beginning of these programs, I explain how I receive the information from the spirit world, how it is interpreted through the inner senses of clairvoyance, clairaudience and clairsentience, and how the language used by spirit beings differs from verbal communication. I also remind the group that in the spirit world, there is no construct of time as we think of it. My reason for informing people about this before I start readings is because, invariably, someone in the group questions why a soul comes through in their reading after passing decades earlier.

For example, suppose Kathy's grandmother, Millie, identifies herself by name and gives a message currently relevant to Kathy's life. Kathy expresses surprise and says, "She passed 30 years ago! You mean she's still connected to me after all this time?" This has happened so frequently in readings that I've decided to give an explanation about this absence of time in the spirit world. In addition to addressing the matter metaphysically, I also mention that because love is eternal, it does not matter whether someone has been gone one day or 30 years; the bond of love endures.

Recently, I gave a group reading in which Linda's mother came through and said that she knew Linda's daughter, Megan, who was born after she had passed. Linda acknowledged this by saying, "I was pregnant with my daughter when my mom passed."

As the communication continued, the mother said that she had been with Megan in the spirit world before she was born. This is a message other spirit beings have delivered through me. Pre-birth relationships exist because we reside in spirit form before we are born. Even if loved ones have passed many years before a child is born, they are still capable of knowing the soul of that child.

Other forms of connection between souls are possible between planes of consciousness. An example of this involves visits from those in spirit during dreams. During these encounters, people report that loved ones appear perfectly happy, healthy and free of pain. In other instances of psychic connections, spirit beings come to family and friends through clairvoyance, by producing scents that were associated with them or by impressing their thoughts on them through intuition and inspiration. The bond of love between souls strengthens this communication. Messages may or may not be given during these encounters; most simply involve the affirmation of the spirit's presence. In all cases that I've heard, people who have these connections say that they've provided reassurance and comfort.

Our association with and love for others in our soul group is a continuation of our prior bond with them. We will meet with them again and again, including between lives in the spirit world. The bond of love we share with our group ensures that it will exist and continue beyond time, space and physical separation. If we genuinely understand this fact, there is no reason to be sad or lonely when we are faced with temporary separations from others through physical circumstances or at the time of death. The heart connection lives on.

In some client readings, it's been evident that love, support and encouragement endure through many generations of families. This is true even though those in prior generations may have never physically met their present-day descendants. Nonetheless, they express an unconditional love for them as family members who carry on positive family traits, the same line of work or creative talents and endeavors.

Jason and his wife, Sharon, both in their early thirties, attended one of my group readings. When I am drawn to them during the program, I immediately notice a curious clairvoyant scene of a man chopping wood in front of a log cabin. I describe this to the couple and tell them that the scene feels as if it were a long time ago. I ask them what this might mean in terms of their ancestors.

"Well, yes, my aunt has done genealogy on my mom's side of the family," Jason responds. "She told me we had ancestors who built their own homes, which were cabins. I think this may be my great-great-grandfather who lived in the south. Of course, I never knew him. I just had a talk with my aunt about this!" he says excitedly.

The man in spirit impresses me with a message to relay to Jason.

"He wants to acknowledge the man who is here in the physical world, the one who works with wood and carpentry. This is someone in your family. I'm not sure who but he says he does a fine job and encourages him in his craft. Do you know who this might be?" I ask.

Jason replies, "This would be my brother, Jim. He builds furniture as a hobby. I can't believe our great-great-grandpa knows about that. That's really cool!"

Other demonstrations of timeless generational love are readings in which sitters' loved ones whom they never knew offer spiritual support for current life challenges—as in the following example.

Olivia, 29, contacts me for guidance and resolution about pressing financial debts she's incurred as a result of losing her job. She asks if it would be possible for me to tune in and do a session that would focus on this practical issue. She is stymied about finding a solution for her financial woes. While on the phone with Olivia, I receive a hunch that someone in spirit wants to connect with her. I advise her to be open to loved ones who might wish to offer wisdom and guidance for her situation. She agrees.

Soon after the session begins, an older woman with gray hair in a bun and a weathered face appears. She's wearing a long dress with an apron and impresses me that she canned fruits and vegetables that her family grew on their farm. I sense her personality of inner strength, fortitude and resiliency. I describe all of this to Olivia.

"Hmm. That sounds like my great-grandmother who died before I was born. My mom has shown me photos of her. What message does she have for me?" Olivia wants to know.

I silently ask the woman her reason for coming through today. "She says she was no stranger to hardships in life, especially during the Great Depression. She gives me the impression that her family worked hard on their farm, but they lost it due to debts owed. They couldn't sustain it and had to move away. In fact, she indicates the family moved around a lot because they couldn't always afford rent."

"Okay, that's too bad," Olivia says. "But what does that have to do with me?"

She's obviously impatient about receiving the answer to her quandary. I tune in and ask the woman what message she is communicating through the images. In a flash of clairaudience, it comes.

"She wants you to know that she is helping you with the very same issue she had in her own life. Her reason for coming through today is to remind you of the qualities of inner strength that have been passed down the generations of your family. She didn't fail and neither will you. She was a survivor and so are you. She says she never lost faith that things would improve."

The spirit woman shows me one of the familiar symbols I use in readings—a rainbow—indicating a happy, peaceful time ahead. I interpret this for Olivia.

"Oh, okay," Olivia responds. "I recall my mom telling me her grandmother struggled in her early life but relied on faith to get her through tough times. So I am to do the same?"

"She overcame many hardships and endured difficult times through fierce determination. Faith and perseverance is what got her through those times. In the end, there is a happy outcome for you, she says. But you must trust that everything works out in the end. Opportunities to clear debt are coming even though you can't see them now. She gives me the impression that you've already planted seeds for positive changes to occur. She will continue to help you through inspiration and your intuition. You'll see things improve, she says."

With this final inspiring message, I feel the woman's presence recede. Olivia says goodbye to me that day in a much lighter mood. Months later, she contacted me for another session and gave me an update about the status of her life.

"I couldn't see it at the time but soon after the reading, I was able to consolidate most of my debt through a new low-interest program I discovered through a friend. It's funny but I hadn't heard about this program before our session even though I had checked many sources. I'm better off now that I'm able to afford monthly payments by working a job another friend referred me to. I'm thankful that my great-grandmother loved me enough to help me. Hearing about her life experiences really encouraged me."

As a medium, I appreciate receiving positive updates about events that transpire in sitters' lives following readings. These are not only intriguing in terms of how messages given by spirit people eventually play out; they also offer, as I spoke of earlier, substantial validation of the bond of love that endures between family members, regardless of generations and the passage of time. Additionally, they serve as reminders of the influential role our ancestors play in our lives decades after they've been gone, another convincing confirmation of our unity with those in our extended soul group.

The Loss of Young Ones

Understanding that we will remain connected with loved ones provides more than comfort. In some cases—particularly with the loss of babies or children (no matter the age)—this truth helps survivors cope with devastating losses. In my readings with parents who have had their children pass into spirit at a young age, I have yet to meet anyone who has not been fundamentally transformed by such deaths. From what they have shared with me, these parents' lives are forever changed by the loss of their children. There are many ups and downs in the aftermath of such deaths.

A frequent message I've given over the years is confirmation of the presence of infants and children (regardless of age of death) with older family members in spirit. As many times as I've been a conduit for these types of messages, I'm still awed by how much comfort and peace they bring to those who receive them.

Because I've never had children, I do not understand firsthand the grief that losing them brings to parents and family members. The closest experience that is comparable for me is the grief I've felt from losing beloved pets who were, to me, like children. To some people, this comparison may seem far-fetched and even disrespectful, but I know many others feel this same way about their animal friends. Grief is grief, no matter the loss. I've frequently witnessed the very same reactions of relief, comfort and gratitude from sitters when I've connected with their cherished pets in readings as from those who connect with children in spirit. So if you have been a "parent" to a pet and have grieved their loss, know that your feelings are perfectly valid and need to be expressed and honored. Take heart in knowing that they, like human children, retain their relationships with you as someone who gave them loving care.

The following story of Katy is representative of various readings in which a sitter's child appears with another family member in spirit.

Katy attended one of my group readings several years ago.

When I connect with her that day, an older woman with an engaging smile and rosy cheeks from Katy's mother's side appears holding a baby girl. I feel her kindness and happiness as she lovingly cuddles the infant. The woman impresses me that she loved babies and children during her physical life. I focus on the spirit woman and tune in further to hear her message for Katy.

"Your grandma on your mother's side wants you to know the baby girl is with her and that she is well cared for." I quickly glance at Katy for validation.

Katy gasps. Her eyes fill with tears. To comfort her, a woman in the group who is sitting beside her hands her a tissue and puts her arm around her. Everyone in the group turns to look at Katy.

I refocus on the older woman in spirit while Katy composes herself. The image of the grandmother and the baby grows more defined in my mind's eye. She obviously needs Katy to validate her presence. I turn back to Katy, waiting for her response. She appears emotionally overwhelmed as she continues to cry. Finally she speaks.

"Three years ago, I lost a daughter who was stillborn. I've never gotten over that. My husband and I were heartbroken. Every day since then, I've asked my grandma to take care of her. It's so good to know my baby is with her," she says, sighing in relief. "She heard my prayer."

At this point, I think the grandmother's message is complete. I expect other relatives of Katy's to come through and to validate their presence. But there is more her grandmother wants to impart. Through clairsentience, she gives me feelings of guilt. Further, she seems to indicate that these feelings need to be addressed. *What could this be about?* I describe what I feel to Katy, hoping it will make sense.

"I've lived with those feelings for three years!" Katy reveals. "You see, I thought I did something to cause my daughter's death. The doctor couldn't give us a solid answer about what happened. Maybe I didn't take good enough care of myself while pregnant. I didn't eat the right foods or rest enough. I convinced myself that her death was my fault. Is my grandma saying it was *not* my fault?"

I ask Katy's grandmother to clarify her message. "Your daughter's passing had nothing whatsoever to do with you personally. It was a tragedy, true, but she lives on in spirit and you will undoubtedly see her again when you return there. Please let go of the guilt that is not serving you. Sometimes, souls only need a brief experience with the physical plane to serve the soul's needs," I explain. "We won't know why that's so until we ourselves return to spirit. I trust this helps," I finish.

Katy appears emotionally drained but immensely relieved to have heard that her grandmother had her child with her. In my mind, I thank the spirit woman who had obviously been aware that Katy was blaming herself for her daughter's death and that she was not at peace. Her grandmother loved her enough to let her know that her baby girl's death was beyond her control. In these types of readings, I am grateful to be a small part of a loving reunion between family members.

For sake of clarification regarding why some souls pass back into spirit at birth or in childhood, my spirit guides tell me that these souls have a karmic imperative to do so because of their pre-birth blueprints. Both birth and death are divinely timed for all souls, regardless of age of death. This is part of the souls' blueprints, as are prearranged agreements with parents. In some cases I've seen, the spiritual lesson necessitates an early physical parting so that parents evolve through having this experience. In other instances, souls need only a brief experience with physicality (for reasons unknown) before returning to the spirit world. In my opinion, it is impossible to know the precise spiritual reason behind these events using the relatively limited perspective of the rational mind. From the soul's elevated vantage point, it knows only expansiveness and eternity.

I'll Be Waiting For You

Nancy greets me pleasantly when she calls my office for her scheduled phone reading. I give her my usual pre-reading information about how the communication operates and advise her to take notes that she can review later. She chuckles nervously and admits to being on edge since this is her first reading. It's common for people to be anxious or overwhelmed when having a reading, especially for the first time. However, anxiety interferes with the efficacy of the reading because it jumbles the lines of communication. A fitting analogy for this is the disruption that occurs when there is static on a telephone line or radio. Emotional, agitated states such as excessive anxiety, anger or sadness weaken the connection. This is why when people make appointments, I advise them to prepare a few questions and engage in stillness, meditation or prayer to calm themselves. This preparation facilitates communication from the spirit world and serves to alleviate their nervousness.

I suggest to Nancy that she take a few deep breaths to release tension. I hear her do so and begin by reciting my usual opening prayer. Before I finish, I become aware of a tall, distinguished-looking man who places himself directly beside Nancy. In my practiced system of mediumship, this placement indicates that he is from the same generation as she. I silently ask him to identify himself by giving more information. He's happy to oblige as the impressions immediately begin to flow.

"There's a tall gentleman who stands next to you. He is dressed in a gray suit with a necktie and wears a dress hat. He places his arm around you and gives me the feeling he is protective of you. I hear the name 'Thomas.' Do you recognize him?"

"Well, that sounds like my deceased husband. He always wore a suit and tie to work and was over six-feet tall. But his name was John, not Thomas," Nancy replies softly.

"Please keep the name of Thomas. It's surely connected somehow," I advise her. (I rarely discard communication from spirit beings, even if sitters initially deny the given evidence. In most cases, these messages are sooner or later validated during the reading or at a later time.)

I pause to receive further information from the man in spirit. He shows me long columns of numbers. The man tells me he had a logical mind and wouldn't have been receptive to seeing a medium when he was here. He comes across as very rationally oriented. I interpret the numbers as related to his work and convey this to Nancy.

"Yes, he was an accountant for a large firm. Oh, he would have never come to see someone like you!" she exclaims laughing. "He was very logical and didn't believe in this sort of thing." She pauses for a moment before adding, "Oh wait! I think I know who Thomas is! He's John's father who passed before him, my father-in-law. Is he telling me he's with his father in spirit then?" Nancy asks.

"Yes and it's also a validation of his father's name," I reply. "He knows I require evidence in readings and that's why he gave his dad's name. He may not have believed in mediumship before he passed, but he does now, he says. By the way, I'm having a sensation of pressure in my chest now. Your husband shows me a symbol of a scar, which means he had a surgical procedure done on his heart. It feels as if something was inserted there at some point. He also says his passing was very quick and there wasn't time to say goodbye to you and others. Does this make sense?"

"Oh, yes!" Nancy replies. "I woke that morning and couldn't rouse him beside me. I panicked and called the local emergency service who tried to revive him but couldn't. He had apparently died during the night. He'd had a pacemaker placed in his heart. We both thought that would give him more time but all of a sudden he was gone. I didn't get to tell him I loved him before he died. I miss him so much." Nancy's voice cracks with emotion.

"He wants you to know he hears you each time you talk to him. He knows how much you miss him because you tell him that all the time, he says. Stop thinking he doesn't hear you because clearly he does! He says you talk to him every night."

I hear Nancy crying softly on the other end of the line. "Yes, that is true. I *do* talk to him. But I've often doubted that he hears me. In fact, that is the very first question I have written right here. Does he know what I ask him every night?"

I mentally ask John this question from his wife. His response comes quickly. I'm flooded by intense feelings of love, which are challenging for me to put into words. He expands this message by giving me an impression of his abiding love for his wife and uses another symbol: a red circle around the words to indicate his emphasis on the message. I do my best to express this to Nancy.

"Your husband loves you deeply. He emphasizes that he will come for you when it's your turn to cross into spirit. He says you've asked him repeatedly to be there for you when that time comes. True?"

"Yes, that is what I ask him every night: to come for me when it's time. I want to be with him when I go over there. I'm stunned that he knew exactly what I've said to him. That's a big relief!"

I receive another symbol from John through clairvoyance: the number 11. He impresses on me that he communicates with Nancy through this number. I relay this to her and ask her the significance of the number.

"I've seen that number so many times since he's passed and wondered if it was a sign from him. Just yesterday I looked at the kitchen clock and saw it was 11:11. Then, when I was driving to the store, the license plate in front of me had 11 on it. Our old house address was 11. You know, his birthday was in November so it could also mean that. That number has much significance to me. Is it really him behind all of this?" Nancy wants to know.

"Apparently, according to what he tells me. It's called **synchronicity**," I explain. "These meaningful coincidences are validation that it's him. He says he'll be sending other signs that you'll notice. Wait and see."

I receive several other messages from John about the couple's grown children before I feel his energy begin to recede. I know it's time to wind down by asking Nancy if she has any questions. After thinking for a moment, she replies.

"This is not a question. I want to thank him and you, Carole, for letting me know he would be there for me, however long it is before I die. You have no idea how much peace it gives me to know this. I'm no longer afraid of being alone and losing John like I've been for months. I know he will always love me just as he did when he was here."

A week or so later, Nancy e-mailed to tell me again how much the reading helped her find peace after her husband's passing. She said that hearing from John during the reading gave her much-needed resolve to enjoy life again. Readings like Nancy's give strong testament to the undying love between spouses who are temporarily separated by the physical world. That part of the relationship has concluded but the spiritual connection lives on. Even though marriage vows contain the phrase "until death do us part", I have seen the opposite to be true, spiritually speaking. We are never parted from those we love. Acceptance of this truth provides comfort and hope to people who open their hearts to receive it.

The next time you feel alone and doubt that your loved ones are aware of how much you love and miss them, remember this: *Nothing* can destroy the bond of love which thrives beyond time and space. There is no reason to be sad. Speak to those in spirit for they will hear you and answer you through your thoughts and feelings. They are assuredly there, right beside you.

Five. Our Power of Choice Determines the Quality of Our Lives

We are the sum total of the decisions we have made.
~ E.A. Bucchianeri

Throughout earlier chapters, I've made frequent reference to the law of karma, or "cause and effect." What we create, we receive. It's true that every cause has an effect and every effect has a cause. All of our thoughts, words and actions eventually return to us. The only variable in this law is the time it takes on the physical plane for the effects of our thoughts, words and actions to manifest.

As I've mentioned previously, all human beings are born with free will and the power of choice as to how that will is used. This is precisely why our ability to choose is so powerful. We get to decide what we will create using our personal will. We make the determination as to what our response to life will be at any given moment. We own the power to create our destiny based on the choices we make, even if the pre-birth lessons of our souls are challenging ones. We make choices that are either inspired by our soul's expression (love and unity) or generated by our mind (fear and separation).

In every imaginable circumstance in life, we have the option to express love or fear. One of my favorite contemporary spiritual teachers, Eckhart Tolle, states it this way: "The primary cause of unhappiness is never the situation but your thoughts about it." (*A New Earth: Awakening to Your Life's Purpose*, Penguin Books, 2008.) What Tolle means here is that events we experience are essentially neutral; it is our *response* to these situations that determines our perception of them and what they offer us in terms of spiritual awareness. We always own the ability to choose our reaction because we have free will. Our response to a given situation is the direct result (effect) of the condition of our consciousness (cause) in that moment. Let's explore this further as it's an important concept.

Thoughts generated by our rational mind are relatively reactive, one-dimensional and limited in comparison to the expanded consciousness of our soul. One of the primal characteristics of the mind is its sensitivity to perceived threats, which could mean injury or death. In an attempt to shield us from these vulnerabilities, the mind puts us on alert by "reacting" to these perceived threats. This reaction is not "wrong"; it's a survival mechanism that's been a core part of our biology during thousands of years of evolution. It's the reason we've even survived as a species. Our brain is wired for self-defense in the almond-shaped part of our brain called the amygdala, which is responsible for survival instincts, emotions and memory. It controls our "fight or flight" responses to perceived dangers. Problems arise, however, when we allow this instinctual part of us to take precedence over the higher consciousness of the soul. Stress contributes to this protective mechanism by sending signals of unease and anxiety—or, "alerts" to the brain. The result is an inability to relax or feel safe in the moment.

The mind perceives threat ("us" versus "them") because it has evolved to protect us. It is not capable of seeing the underlying unity and interconnectedness of all. Most (if not all) of humanity's troubles have been and are presently rooted in this single illusion of separation, which originates from rational, defensive thinking. Instead of perceiving our commonality with others, we see our differences. Truly knowing that we are one with all others eliminates anger, prejudice and hatred, which are all generated from fear. Unfortunately, these toxic emotions are rampant in the current polarized political climate of the United States, and in other parts of the world. This schism is the direct result (the effect) of our own misconstrued perceptions about our spiritual unity with others (the cause). To bring about cohesiveness where separation currently exists, we must change our thoughts from division and separation to cooperation and unity. Although this sounds like a daunting task, I believe we can succeed if we allow it. This change must first take place within each of us.

So how and where do we begin? To tune into the wisdom of the soul, we must go beyond the mind. Meditation, stillness, breath focus and spending time in nature are pathways to this higher awareness. Stilling the incessant flow of thoughts from our rational mind opens the door to expanded, limitless consciousness. Accessing this higher state regularly leads to less fear-based choices and responses. When viewed from this vantage point, we gain fresh perspectives about problems, tap our intuition and experience inner peace.

The spirit world teaches that we are personally responsible for all the choices we make. This is true since we alone own our personal will. We enjoy the rewards of peace and happiness for positive choices or suffer pain and unhappiness for harmful ones. Time is immaterial when considering the effects our choices create; once energy is put forth in the form of thoughts, words and actions, it is guaranteed to return to us sooner or later.

Cause, Effect and Natural Laws

As we started to discuss in earlier chapters, the law of karma (like all natural laws) operates regardless of our awareness of or belief in it. Natural laws are impartial, impersonal and immutable—meaning they are valid, invariable and true, regardless of our awareness of them, who we are (race, economic status, nationality) and where we reside geographically. This irrelevance of location is an important distinction between natural laws and man-made ones. With the latter, as we know, a law may apply and be enforced in one area and not in another, based on the beliefs, whims and dictates of those residing in the area and those who create the laws.

For example, recreational marijuana is currently legal in 10 states in America as of January 2019 because the voters and legislators in those states now deem it so. In the 40 others, it is illegal because it has not (yet) been approved by residents and lawmakers. Another example is the disparity in gun laws. Some states permit certain types of firearms and others do not. Possessing a banned weapon in one state results in fines or imprisonment, whereas the possession of the same firearm in another is not prosecuted. These types of variations based on prevailing thoughts and opinions do not exist in natural laws; they apply equally to all people and all circumstances.

For many years, I've created and taught workshops on various topics related to metaphysics. In one class about natural laws, I illustrated the concept of the constancy of these universal principles by using the analogy of gravity, a physical law. For example, if I drop a pencil, would it fail to hit the floor because of my personal refusal to believe in the law of gravity? Of course it would fall, regardless of my belief. The same is true of natural laws. I've considered that if people who commit crimes knew without a doubt that every harmful action they take has an equally negative guaranteed consequence to them, the world would probably be far better and safer than it is. Crimes of all types would be significantly reduced, although there would undoubtedly still be those who attempt to outwit this natural law.

I've encountered people who refute the existence of natural laws. In my opinion, they do so because they give too much weight to the construct of time. That is, since the *effect* produced by the *cause* (thoughts, words and actions) may be delayed in the physical plane, they believe the law is invalid, an erroneous conclusion. The fact is that our personal choices made through free will *always* produce effects. In some cases, those effects may not be evident until much later in life or in future incarnations.

The late American psychic and trance medium Edgar Cayce gave many readings in which he told people they were currently reaping the effects of choices (causes) made in previous incarnations. These sitters came to Cayce seeking counsel on why particular physical, emotional or mental issues plagued them. By reading their Akashic files, Cayce was able to access the root thoughts that created the current challenges, circumstances or maladies. He then prescribed "remedies" that people could use to balance those thoughts and heal their bodies. These remedies were sometimes physical (specific foods, vitamins, minerals and elixirs), spiritual (replacing disharmonious and fear-based thoughts with spiritually centered ones of love, faith and peace) or a combination of both. They were intended to lift the energy vibration of individuals to achieve healing. For more on Cayce's life, his readings and the remedies he prescribed, read *Edgar Cayce: The Sleeping Prophet* by Jess Stearn (Doubleday, 1967) and *The Edgar Cayce Remedies* by Dr. William A. McGarey (Bantam Books, 1983).

As I mentioned earlier in terms of suicide, some spirit beings communicate how they would make different choices than they did in life, retrospectively. After seeing their life reviews, they are aware of how the choices they made affected the quality of life they lived and, importantly, how those choices affected others.

The Power of Choice Resides Within You

Who doesn't want control over one's life? Interestingly, there are those who choose to *not* determine the direction and quality of their own lives. This stems from two causes:

First, some people falsely assume they must please others (spouses, family, friends and peers) at all costs to their own happiness. I believe this has been especially true for women, although that is thankfully changing nowadays. For these people, it is much less risky—in the interest of gaining and keeping others' approval—to dismiss making their own choices in favor of going along with society's and others' expectations of them. Sooner or later, this refusal of personal power leads to unhappiness, stagnancy and suffering in one form or another. It is not possible to be untrue to oneself for long, although some people awaken more quickly than others. Living without authenticity always backfires in the end. Further, people often build resentments from continually disowning their power of choice. Unfortunately, these resentments are often projected onto the very people whose approval they sought in the first place in an attempt to save face or to play the role of victim. Blaming others for our own failure to make choices fosters anger, bitterness, dependency and more failure.

Every so often, I've seen an online article that lists the top 10 regrets of people who were dying. First on the list is "living to please others and not following one's own dreams." If we do not live true to self, we regret that choice in the end. Trying to fit in with the hope of gaining others' approval denies and suppresses the soul's unique expression. This form of self-sabotage and undervaluing of oneself never leads to our soul's path of happiness and freedom. We can be no one other than who we are without compromising or losing our self-worth.

The second reason some people do not take control over the direction of their lives and make intentional choices is because they fear doing so. This fear can come in various forms, including subconsciously avoiding choice because of the fear of making the wrong choice. Some are afraid of how drastically their lives may change when they assert their choices, especially if those choices take them down unfamiliar pathways. Most of us fear the unknown because we have become comfortable with the known, however stifling, unfulfilling or horrible that may be. For example, if I am afraid of being alone, I remain in an unloving or abusive relationship because it's preferable to being by myself. In another instance, if I fear I'm not smart, qualified or talented enough to land my dream career, I'll settle for a less fulfilling job because I fear failure in the dream career. In both of these common situations, I have seen how people tend to blame others, outer circumstances or fate for their unhappiness. Since our thoughts create our reality, self-defeating ones lead to feelings of unworthiness, helplessness, depression and, in some cases, physical illness.

As far as making the wrong choice, fear of failure sabotages those who do not view it as an opportunity to learn and grow. With a mindset geared towards perfectionism, some people resist making choices because they believe they will not be the right ones. So they do nothing then complain that life is unfulfilling, stagnant or passing them by. Many life choices involve risk with the potential of making mistakes; but mistakes are only such if we fail to learn from them. If we use them to grow spiritually, they become assets. As popular 12-step recovery programs state in their literature, "We claim spiritual progress rather than spiritual perfection." (*The Big Book of Alcoholics Anonymous* by Dr. Bob Smith and Bill Wilson, CreateSpace Independent Publishing Platform; First Edition, 2013.)

Regarding choice and personal responsibility in readings, I've reminded sitters of the truth about their own free will numerous times. Surprisingly, this simple fact of their ownership of free will may never have occurred to them or if it has, they choose to dismiss it. I've been contacted by people who are eager to hand over their power of choice to me during their readings. This is more common when sessions involve life guidance rather than mediumship. As I mentioned earlier, usually these people want me to tell them what to do in a career or relationship situation. In these cases, I've responded that I cannot and will not be responsible for the choices they make; the most I can do is give insights about the energy I perceive around the situation. Each time this happens, I'm thankful that I honor ethics in my practice because this scenario is exactly how people can be easily exploited. It's never a wise idea to subjugate your power of personal choice to someone else.

Because of my adherence to ethics, I have turned away individuals whom I sensed were contacting me for too many sessions within a short period of time. I've flat out told them that they are seeking answers outside of themselves instead of looking within. Believe it or not, some of them have argued with me about the matter, although I've refused to give in.

Creating and supporting dependency in others—in any circumstance—is extremely unhealthy emotionally and leads to negative karma for both parties. It's incredibly important to me to be honest with people about what I can and cannot do. A good reading in terms of life guidance should not be a "power trip" for a medium or the recipient. Instead, it is a signpost that points in the direction and support of harmonious living from a spiritually centered perspective. In addition, it should encourage empowerment for sitters. I've often shared that if you go to a psychic or medium who tells you what to do as far as choice, run far away from that person!

Spirit Cannot Decide For You

Another topic I've addressed in my practice is that of deceased family members and friends, spirit guides, angels and spirit teachers dictating choice to people. None of these beings can tell us what we should do regarding life situations because they are aware of the principle of free will. No one in spirit can make decisions for us. Occasionally, people will say that their spirit guides told them to do this or that. I've reminded them that they are probably confusing the voice of their own mind with that of their guides. The role of spirit guides, angels and teachers involves their agreement to help on our spiritual path while we are on the physical plane. That does not usurp our personal responsibility. Guides will always come through to us using a loving tone, which honors our soul and not our ego. To build trust in intuitive messages you receive personally (without a medium or psychic), always check the content and tone of that message. Does the message serve your soul or stroke your ego? Promptings from the soul will always support your spiritual awareness and growth.

Choices Help to Build Trust

People occasionally contact me for guidance when they feel indecisive about a particular area of life like career, relationships, health, spirituality or financial matters. In many cases, fear about making a wrong choice is the cause of their inertia. Eradicating that fear substantially diminishes the anxiety that accompanies decision making. If we understand that "wrong" choices do not really exist, we can move ahead more confidently. If we trust that we are here to learn and grow, we also know that "mistakes" are opportunities. Here's why:

A soul comes to earth to express and experience itself in the world of form. As it does so, it never loses awareness of its true identity as Spirit: loving, nonjudgmental and divine. This is the real, eternal, expansive essence of who we are. Tuning into our soul's consciousness, where *all* experiences are equally valid, builds trust and reassurance that even wrong choices teach us something of value about ourselves if we are open to learning.

The human side of us perceives limitation, imperfections and "wrong" choices. We judge right from wrong as a necessary thing to do; however, the mind continually judges experiences from a relatively narrow perspective—namely, a self-centered one. If we choose to temporarily suspend the mind's judgment when faced with decisions, fear and stress are reduced. When faced with choice, considering possibilities that exist within a situation allows us to remain open to our intuition and its guidance. This does not mean that we shouldn't gather information and consider it when faced with decision making; but once that is done, we must trust that we've done the best we can and turn to the higher intuition of our soul. Below is an example of this type of guidance, delivered by a young woman's grandmother in spirit.

Carlie, 25, calls my office for a phone reading. She tells me that she has no particular interest in hearing from relatives in spirit, but instead needs guidance on a specific issue. She says she currently feels stuck and is torn between quitting her unfulfilling job (which she's hesitant to leave for financial reasons), finding another job she likes better or possibly returning to school, which would necessitate her moving home with her parents. She had completed two years of college, quit and started working. Now she wants to know which direction would be best for her.

"I know you don't care if you hear from anyone in spirit, but sometimes they have other ideas," I explain to her before I begin. "If someone in spirit has guidance to offer, don't be closed to it. Let's see if anyone cares to step in and help you."

Sure enough, as I recite my opening prayer, I become aware of an older, stout woman with a walker standing on Carlie's right (maternal) side. She shows me her weathered hands, a symbol I use to indicate a person who's worked hard in a physical job. Further, she impresses on me that she had severe arthritis in her spine. I relay all of this to Carlie with the hope that she will recognize the woman.

"That's my grandma, Mildred," Carlie exclaims. "She passed away when I was only two. My mom told me she had lots of back pain. What message does she have?"

"Mildred says she worked very hard from a young age. She had to go to work when she was in her early teen years after her father passed. She cleaned houses and later worked in a factory. The dreams she had of going to college were never realized because of financial obstacles. She impresses on me that the reason she comes through to you is that she wants to remind you that you have options. She encourages you with your education. You see, she did not have that choice since she had to work to support her family. She wants to remind you that you *do* have choices."

"But can she tell me what to do about my job?" Carlie asks impatiently. "I need to know whether to stay or quit and go back to school."

"She cannot tell you what to do, Carlie. That's not her purpose for coming to you. What she is saying is that she had no choice in her situation, but you do. You have the freedom to make choices and that, in itself, is a blessing. You won't fail if you learn something about yourself in this situation. Taking risks is part of being human. You must follow your gut."

I pause as Mildred relays another impression, one that is circled in red through my inner vision—a sign indicating the message is of particular importance.

"She says you need to have faith that you will make the right choice for your life. You don't trust your own judgment enough because you're too worried about making a mistake. The other thought she imparts to me is that women in those days had few opportunities as you do today. So she was stuck in a sense, but you aren't. She didn't graduate high school, did she?"

"Um, I don't think she did," Carlie responds. "Does she say which choice would be better for me?" she asks insistently.

"Carlie, you're having this reading because you thought you were stuck, right?"

"Well, yes. I go round and round in my mind about what to do. I can't seem to choose what to do so I do nothing. It's very frustrating. I'm so afraid of making a mistake," she finally admits. "Can't my grandma see which choice is better for me?"

It's clear that fear of failure is holding Carlie back from moving forward. She has little trust in herself or Spirit. This is what her grandmother is attempting to communicate to her, but she isn't getting it. I decide to communicate Mildred's message another way so she can grasp it.

"Look, a life without risk is comforting to imagine, but you will not grow much that way. Your soul came to earth to learn and evolve in its unique way and under certain sets of circumstances. Mildred encourages you to take advantage of choices, despite your fear of making wrong ones. The point is to develop trust in your own internal guidance, which comes from your soul. Any choice you make will teach you more about yourself. You can't and won't lose."

"Okay. I get it!" Carlie replies with a sigh. "I'm going to work on that fear and learn to trust more. I appreciate that my grandma came through today. I feel as if I know her better now. Thank you, Carole."

"Thank *her*," I reply. "Even though you never got to know her on earth, she is your ancestor and a member of your spiritual family. You'll fail only if you give up and do nothing. Trust that you won't make a wrong decision in this situation."

A few years later, I heard from Carlie. She had returned to college and earned a degree in counseling. She told me that after our session, she was inspired intuitively to quit her job, move home and resume her education. Grateful to follow her soul's calling, she was working in a mental health facility that specialized in treating children and adolescents. I'm sure her grandmother in spirit is proud of her for following her dream and finally leaving fear behind.

The Danger of Victim Mentality

Victim mentality is the mistaken belief that one is repeatedly the recipient of bad circumstances. This self-defeating thinking denies the reality of choice and responsibility for the state of one's own life. Because we have the ability to make choices about how we respond to anything in life, the idea that we are destined to be at the mercy of events or others is untrue. Sure, unfortunate events beyond our control will likely occur at some point in our lives but taking on a victim mentality about such events leads to further victimhood. That is, we become victims of our own thoughts of powerlessness about being a victim! Life can take surprising twists and turns that we don't see coming or elude our rational understanding. This does not mean, however, that we are powerless when faced with these circumstances. We can choose how to respond to them. In fact, our ability to choose our reaction to anything in life is the most valuable asset we own. I can't stress that enough.

Victim mentality includes blaming others who may have nothing whatsoever to do with the situation. It can create resentment, anger and stress, as well as mental and physical illness. I've personally seen how this type of thinking destroys relationships and fractures families. I've had many sessions in which siblings have gone years without speaking to one another, parents are estranged from their children and generations of families harbor grudges over long-forgotten resentments. In my experience, few people own their part in causing or carrying on these divisive situations. They instead succumb to identifying with victimhood, which closes off any chance of reconciliation. In some of these readings, spirit communicators come through and not only acknowledge the situation, but also advise loved ones that they need to stop blaming others for whatever the problem is. Through viewing the situation from an expanded perspective, these souls know how spiritually damaging victim mentality is and they want to impart that wisdom to their families.

Once in spirit, all self-deception and illusion fall away since we no longer have a rational mind to generate them. We see the truth of what we thought, felt and did. In cases where spirit beings passed as a result of poor personal choices, they communicate that truth to sitters. Since there are really no "good" or "bad" choices according to the soul's perspective, I believe the intent behind this type of message is to prevent or reduce the suffering that accompanies self-defeating choices.

They want to help us avoid needless pain that they themselves endured because of poor choices.

I have heard from spirit beings who acknowledge their responsibility for unhealthy behaviors such as eating poorly, smoking heavily, drinking excessively and taking drugs. On other occasions, I've connected with those who admit that they should have taken better care of their health by going for medical checkups and heeding medical advice. Some mention that if they had not stubbornly refused the helpful recommendations of family and friends, they could have benefited from that advice.

At times, I've felt as though I am witnessing "true confessions" from the spirit world. During one session, a man in spirit who had been severely diabetic prior to death told his wife that he should have stayed on the diet he had been prescribed instead of secretly eating cookies, candy and desserts. She had warned him many times (he admitted this in the reading) but he chose to ignore her. Needless to say, he expressed his regrets to her about his unwise choices.

In some cases, spirits take responsibility for engaging in foolish acts that led to their deaths, such as texting while driving or speeding and causing an accident. Because sitters sometimes come with questions about loved ones' behaviors, actions and emotional states prior to dying, these types of messages can be particularly healing for them. I've also delivered numerous messages where spirit beings express concern over someone in the physical world making the same wrong choices as they did, like having an affair or remaining in an unhealthy relationship. They see the reading as an opportunity to help others make better choices to avoid future tragedies.

A common tenet of metaphysical spirituality is that there are no victims in life. This is true as we've discussed in Part One. Souls sign up for life experiences before birth, although few remember doing so; but I believe this truth has been misunderstood by those who distort it by blaming others for unpleasant situations and events. In other words, this misinterpretation assumes that people consciously create their own hardships and therefore are undeserving of compassion or help. Nothing could be farther from the truth. We should never judge or blame anyone who is suffering in any way. Both compassion and assistance need to be extended in these circumstances.

A good illustration of this faulty perception is when people blame others for being ill. Years ago, I participated in various spiritual groups where some members made sanctimonious comments about people being responsible for creating their own illnesses. This judgment presumes that we know the underlying factors about others' lessons, their personal thoughts, emotions and experiences when we clearly don't. We are fortunate to have glimpses of our own karmic lessons. While it may be true that souls contract to experience certain illnesses, certainly most people do not consciously choose to be sick. Showing compassion is always the right choice to make.

Free Will and Windows of Opportunity

Throughout life, we are continually presented with opportunities to use our free will. **Windows of opportunity** are situations that present us with the option of mending and/or releasing old ways of thought and being. They are portals to higher awareness where we view life from a vantage point above our own entrenched thoughts, beliefs and conditioned, habitual reactions. These are pivotal, life-changing moments that give us chances to discard self-limiting thoughts and embrace loving, compassionate ones instead.

Importantly, they lead us to open our hearts more deeply, if we so choose. Throughout many readings I've given, spirit beings reference these circumstances to sitters so they can recognize them—as in this example:

Ron is a tall, tan, muscular man in his late fifties. He sits down on the small couch in my reading room and removes his ball cap. He tells me he owns a construction company and hands me a business card. The deep expression lines on his forehead are accentuated in the glow of the table lamp beside him. He appears weary.

"I've never seen a medium before but I'm interested in what you have to say," he announces. "I don't want anyone in my family to know I'm here today," he says firmly. "They don't believe in this."

I assure him the session is confidential. I sense that he, too, is skeptical about mediumship yet is searching for answers about something very troubling. I soon discover what that is.

Immediately upon tuning in, I sense the presence of a young woman with short, dark hair and a tattoo of a butterfly on her right arm. Without hesitation, Ron confirms her as his daughter, Leah, whom he says passed less than a year prior.

Instead of giving details about the manner of her death, Leah bombards me with an abundance of emotions: sadness, confusion, anger and isolation. I silently ask her to slow down so that I can relate these to her dad. I'm surprised that she doesn't give details of her death (which spirits normally do) but I adjust my expectations and go with the flow. The young woman impresses me with feelings of insistency around giving a message to her father.

"Your daughter wants to talk about the two of you being estranged before her passing," I begin. "When I connect with her, she gives me feelings of being alienated by and estranged from her family. I get the sense she moved away from her family because she wanted to maintain distance. She gives me feelings of sadness and anger. I'm not sure what this means. She says she felt alone, confused and that no one understood her. Does this make sense to you, Ron?" I ask, looking directly at him.

Ron clears his throat. The shocked expression on his face is impossible for me to ignore, although I usually train my focus on the communicating spirits. He obviously didn't anticipate the directness of the message, especially at the very start of the reading. He averts his eyes to the wall behind me then shifts his gaze downward. Finally he replies.

"Um, yeah, it does make sense," he stammers. "I disowned my daughter because she was gay. That's a sin, according to my faith. We weren't speaking at the time of her death. What does she have to say about it now?" His tone is callous, cold.

There's a sense of urgency in Leah's message to her father that I know I must impart to him. I keep the link with her strong by mentally interviewing her about her life. She begins to tell me her story through a series of impressions.

"Leah says she wrestled with her feelings about being gay for a long time. She knew in her heart that you would not approve of her life but she loved you as her dad. For a long time, she hid her true self from you and others in the family to get along and to keep the peace. She was overwhelmed by the constant inner tension this created. She wasn't being true to herself. That's why she turned to using drugs. It feels as if she had an overdose from an opiate, but it wasn't intentional," I finish.

It now makes sense to me why Leah had held off talking about how she died at the beginning of the reading. She wants to explain the reason behind her overdose; how it relates to the emotional pain she had endured. I pause to let this register with Ron. His eyes remain downcast but I know he's listening intently, although he says nothing. I also know there's more Leah wants to say to him.

"She says that she's now aware that she came as a teacher to help open your heart as far as having understanding for others. During her life review, she saw that she and you had planned this, even though you don't remember that. Please, she says, don't miss this opportunity to change your thoughts about differences in others. Open your mind and heart! There's no need for guilt about her death as long as you see the lesson contained in it."

I glance at Ron who appears annoyed, confounded, irritated and frustrated by this message. Intuitively, I'm aware of the tension he's feeling. He sits silently staring at the ball cap in his lap. At this point, I sense the presence of his spirit guide who wants to communicate wisdom to further validate what his daughter has said.

"Your spirit guide steps in here and says Leah's death presents you with the chance to let go of judgments. As painful as it is to lose a child, especially one you were not speaking to, don't let this window of opportunity to open your heart pass you by. You can make the choice to see the goodness in her and the underlying unity of everyone, instead of focusing on their differences. The truth is that we are all children of Spirit, regardless of religion. Please think about this."

Ron sighs heavily but does not utter a word. The tension in the room is palpable. Clearly, he's uncomfortable with all of this. *Is this having an impact on him?* I wonder. *I hope so.*

Leah gives several other evidential messages about her life, which Ron validates by simply nodding. She wants her mother to know she's aware of a recent illness and that she loves her. She knows her brother recently took a new job. The session concludes with these messages. Ron sighs heavily again, stands up and puts his cap back on his head.

As he extends his hand to me, I look him squarely in the eyes and suggest he give the reading time to sink in without judgment about what was communicated.

"I have a lot to think about. I never understood Leah," Ron says with a sigh. "From the time she was a little girl, she was different from my other kid, my son. I never expected to hear this when I came here tonight," he says, shaking his head. "I guess I didn't think it would be possible for Leah to reach me through you, but how would you have known any of this otherwise? Part of me wishes I *hadn't* heard it since it forces me to make a choice between following my religion and being at peace with my child. I'll give it some thought. I do feel some relief. Well, anyway, thank you," he says matter-of-factly. He moves toward the door to leave.

"Your daughter loves you and that is why she came here tonight," I say. "Open your heart. She'll know when you do, believe me."

Although Ron's tragic scenario is one most people will thankfully never have to face, it is not extraordinary in its universal message of taking the opportunity to rise above fear and judgment by following the calling of our soul, which is love. In Ron's case, his judgment of his daughter separated him from her, physically and emotionally when she was alive and spiritually after her death. Although her death brought Ron sorrow, all was not lost. As Leah pointed out during the reading, he now had the chance to view the situation from a higher perspective by choosing different thoughts, releasing the past and softening his heart.

Windows of opportunity serve our spiritual growth by giving us the chance to reinvent ourselves. The moment we make the choice to release the past, we begin the journey of healing. Forgiveness is so vital to this process that I've dedicated an entire chapter to the topic (Chapter 8). Windows of opportunity are potential escape routes from our own illusions of separation from others. Opening them allows the higher consciousness of love to radiate through the darkness of fear, resentment, anger, hatred, false pride and judgment. Reconciling past hurts leads to profound inner transformation.

By understanding that we carry the light of Spirit within, we are naturally led to express what that light is comprised of: the energy of love. It is our choice and personal responsibility to align ourselves with principles that reawaken our soul's highest purpose: to give and receive love. By doing this, we see others and ourselves with fresh vision. When we identify with love, we come home to the comforting presence of Spirit.

Six. Life Values Transcend Death

Don't let your special character and values, the secret that you know and no one else does—the truth—don't let that get swallowed up by the great chewing complacency.

~ Aesop

Long before I delved into spiritual studies, I thought I knew what was important in life. In my teens and early twenties, no one could convince me that anything could possibly be more vital to my happiness than having money to go to bars and parties with eccentric friends, attending rock concerts, wearing trendy, offbeat clothes and engaging in superficial, romantic relationships. During those years, I had no concept whatsoever of inner values, let alone the purpose and meaning of my life. My priorities consisted of entertaining myself with fleeting pleasures and making sure I never, ever removed the façade I hid behind. Instant gratification was the name of the game for me, and the quicker the better. In those days, I was a lost soul who sought solace and escape in the next alluring adventure that happened to pop into my existence. By the age of 25, I was headed straight, as they say, "down the tubes." I was extraordinarily successful at one thing only: creating suffering for myself and, at times, others.

It was the early 1980s when I entered a 12-step program and private therapy for recovery from alcohol abuse, which forced me to strip away the pretentious mask I had long worn. There was no denying that I had to face the self-destructive patterns I'd allowed to take over my life. During this time, I began to explore inner values, positive priorities and pathways to awaken to something more profound in life. I wasn't certain what that was, but I soon realized that I needed to transform spiritually if I was to have any hope of recovery and straightening out my life. This intense journey of self-discovery began in the rooms of those 12-step group meetings and private counseling sessions. I discovered that I had to eradicate my old ways of thinking and replace them with fresh, healthy values. The superficial things I had been holding so dear weren't serving me. In fact, they were killing me. I had no one to blame for the abysmal state of my life; it was all my doing.

For a decade or so, one day at a time, I sought to connect with Spirit within myself instead of earthly, outside sources as I had been doing. Somewhere along the way, I realized the immense value of humility and gratitude, qualities stressed in the 12-step teachings. These are ones I needed to embrace. Working the steps of the recovery program instilled me with the values of faith, hope and trust. I also made new friends whom I respected for their wisdom, stability and reliability. A new perspective on life was being birthed within me, one that prioritized uplifting, lasting values that would lead to spiritual and personal fulfillment.

This "recovery" from self-centered thinking and behavior continues today, enhanced and supported by meditation, prayer, service and every reading I give. Looking back at the person I was 35 years ago, I can hardly believe that shell of a person was me. Only through the grace and love of Spirit is such radical healing possible. Only through living a spiritually centered life that embraces divine qualities such as love, compassion and service can we move beyond fear, pain and self-serving behaviors. Only when we truly commit ourselves to the presence of Spirit within ourselves do we realize the expansive vision of our soul and know our true purpose. I will forever be grateful for the meaningful foundation 12-step programs provided for me.

In various sessions, spirit beings communicate messages about priorities and values in life that apply to everyone. It's interesting to note that few of these communications have a religious tone or involve a specific philosophy. Instead, they focus on universal values common to most human beings: love of family, friendship, compassion, gratitude, generosity, honesty, integrity, freedom, patience and service. These qualities emphasize the interconnectedness of all, regardless of outward differences and religious beliefs. They speak to the underlying, genuine spirituality that unites all souls.

I refer to spirit beings who communicate this type of universal wisdom as **teaching spirits**. In these types of communications, spirits often use the example of their own lives to impart specific wisdom to sitters who they knew while on earth. Their mission is to relay the importance of these values to family and friends. Although they may not have that formal title or role, teaching is precisely what they do in communicating messages about important, spiritual qualities during readings.

In this chapter, I discuss the values of gratitude, compassion and service because they frequently surface during readings. Regularly practicing these core qualities instills inner peace, emotional fulfillment, well-being, empathy and enhanced satisfaction in relationships.

Giving Thanks Increases Spirit's Grace and Abundance

At the start of a memorable reading I gave to Edie, a personal care nurse, an unexpected spirit came through to impart a meaningful message that made an impact on both her and me. His communication beautifully illustrates the elevated quality of gratitude.

"An older gentleman with salt and pepper hair appears here in a wheelchair," I relay to Edie. "He mentions the name 'Jerry.' Do you recognize him?"

Edie appears stumped by this description. "I'm not sure. Let me think for a minute."

I tune in to get more information. The man impresses me with a neurological condition that affected his entire body, including his speech. I see him sitting in the wheelchair alone, gazing out a window. After passing all of this along to Edie, her face suddenly lights up in recognition.

"Oh, wait! That's Jerry, the man I took care of for two years over a decade ago. I was a private duty nurse in those days and he was my patient. He had Parkinson's disease and couldn't speak clearly prior to his death. What does he say?"

I'm as surprised by Jerry's presence as Edie obviously is. He's not a relative or friend. *Why is he here today?* I ask him his reason for coming through to Edie. He impresses me through clairsentience with strong gratitude for her care of him and that he considered her family because he had been alone near the end of his life. She had been his lifeline in his final years. The feelings are so intense it almost overwhelms me. I tear up. (I usually remain detached emotionally from the communication during readings, but sometimes it's nearly impossible to not feel the depth of emotion when certain messages are brought through. This is one of those times.)

"He says he is thankful for your care. That is the reason he came today." I look at Edie sitting quietly across from me, hoping I did justice in communicating the man's sincere message of gratitude.

She smiles. "I understand now. You see, Jerry had no one else to depend on but me. He had no children and his wife had already passed. I did nursing duties but I also read to him, sang and held his hand when he was afraid. The illness impaired his thinking and he was often anxious and upset. How nice of him to come and thank me. Can you tell him I remember him fondly?"

"He says he knows you think of him," I reply. "People in spirit hear our thoughts. You can communicate with him through your thoughts directly, without me. He came through today because he wanted to make sure you knew how grateful he was for your care, and that you would hear that loud and clear. It may not have been a big deal to you, he says, but it made a huge difference to him."

I can tell Edie is moved by Jerry's touching message. The rest of the hour-long reading consists of lively, validating messages from Edie's parents in spirit, as well as several aunts and uncles who make references to childhood memories.

After the session concludes, I'm struck with another impression from Jerry's earlier communication. This one comes from Edie's own spirit guides. I decide to pass it along to her.

"You know, I can't help but feel that Jerry's message of thanks is a powerful reminder to you of the difference you make in people's lives. Your guides want you to remember that. We all need that kind of reminder now and then because we can get burned out by our work. Think about that. By doing what you do with nursing, you help people more than you realize."

"Yes, I suppose that's true," she replies softly. "I have been feeling burned out by my work lately. How could you have known that? I'm grateful Jerry came to me today. What a gift!"

Edie's reading gives me pause to reflect on how seemingly small gestures make a positive difference in another's life. Because of Jerry's message of gratitude, I've become more aware of how I can practice gratitude in my own life. I believe we receive exactly what we need when we need it. Jerry's message has inspired me to engage in my own personal practice of gratitude.

The reading with Edie also reminds me that it's important to thank people for their help, kindness and service whenever possible. Expressing gratitude intensifies our connection with Spirit by elevating our consciousness to affirm life's abundance. Simply stated, gratitude is the appreciation of both small and large blessings in life. From the food we eat to the relationships we hold dear, there are a multitude of things to be thankful for. When we acknowledge the good things we already have in life, the stage is set energetically for more good things to flow to us. When we acknowledge the unlimited resources of Spirit, we attract more of those resources. By contrast, if we see only what's wrong in life, we shut the door on the higher vibration of consciousness that's necessary to attract positive experiences and events. This is assured by another natural law: the **law of attraction**, which states that like energy attracts like energy. Because thoughts are energy, we attract people, situations and things that match our predominant thoughts.

Even small, seemingly insignificant gestures are worthy of gratitude. Two years ago, I was going through a particularly difficult time emotionally. One day, as I was in the checkout line at a store, I engaged in small talk with the friendly, kind cashier. As we chatted, I was grateful for her presence and attention. At the time, I'm sure she had no idea that our brief conversation served as the perfect refreshing, lighthearted connection I needed at that time. When I headed to my car that day, I felt uplifted. I noticed that my cares and worries were not nearly as vexing as before. In that moment, I thanked Spirit for placing the woman on my pathway that day. She clearly made a positive impact on me when I most needed it. A few weeks afterwards, I thanked her personally, an opportunity I didn't want to pass by. Just as I had presumed, she was surprised but grateful for my thanks. Perhaps my gratitude made a difference in her life, something I may never know.

Being thankful for others' contributions to our lives, however large or small they may be, validates the person's efforts and strengthens our relationship with Spirit, the source of all abundance. I've lost count of how often the simple message of thanks has been expressed by spirits such as Jerry in Edie's reading. These communications are expressions of appreciation from one soul to another, which brings healing to both. The messages also bring inspiration, encouragement and confirmation to those who receive them. Of course, this is true not only during readings but throughout life. It doesn't matter if souls exist in the physical or spirit world; giving thanks to another for their presence or service is always a rewarding experience for both parties.

Gratitude transforms us spiritually because it replaces thoughts of lack with those of abundance. It accentuates the positive aspects of life, which leads to personal fulfillment. Psychological studies in recent years confirm that when people focus on gratitude, remarkable changes occur in their lives, including relief from mild depression and anxiety, and improved overall physical health.

Valuing people and pets over things seems to bring the most health benefits. An easy way to practice this is to go into a quiet space and think about the specific quality a cherished person or pet brings into your life. What does that gift mean to you? Feel it deeply. To make these thoughts more concrete, write them down. Notice how your body feels when you think thoughts of gratitude. When I have practiced this, I feel relaxation and peace wash over me. Stress is noticeably reduced. Negative thoughts such as anger, envy and resentment dissipate. My heart feels fuller.

Gratitude is thankfulness for the outpouring of grace and kindness from others. The expression "the grace of God" refers to the immeasurable kindness and loving care that flows from Spirit to every living being. Gratitude is the grace that we return to Spirit for blessings received. It is the kindness that emanates from our heart when we acknowledge and give thanks for the blessings and goodness we receive from that universal source. (Interesting side note: I'm writing these thoughts on gratitude as Thanksgiving approaches this week, a fun synchronicity!)

Compassion and Higher Consciousness

From the Latin root *compati* ("to suffer with"), compassion means to feel the suffering of another. Feeling compassion for another emphasizes the connection we share with all living beings, regardless of external differences. It is empathy, care and concern that inspires and motivates us to help alleviate the suffering of others. Compassionate gestures are among the most selfless, considerate and encouraging gifts we can offer. In doing so, we raise our consciousness to assimilate unconditional love, selflessness and heart-centered service. Everyone benefits when compassion moves us to genuinely understand and reach out to others in need. It's the compelling force that inspires and drives service, enables us to care enough to initiate positive changes in the world and love others as ourselves. It is fundamental to humanity's physical and spiritual evolution. Compassion brings assurance that no one is truly alone in suffering; it is a human condition we all have at some point.

Years of practicing mediumship have given me a profound sensitivity to the suffering of others, so much so that detachment is a requirement for doing my work or I risk being ineffective as a conduit and possibly getting ill. As mentioned previously, most of the time I am successful at this, but there are exceptions in particularly touching readings. As medium John Holland says in his training course on mediumship, "The price of sensitivity [as a conduit] *is* sensitivity [to life]."

When I reflect on my life before doing readings, I become even more grateful for the gift of compassion, which has greatly intensified as a direct result of my work. Feeling compassion for people who suffer from grief and other troubling emotions has enabled me to grow spiritually, which is my overarching goal. I've also developed compassion for all living beings because each is Spirit in form. Simply stated, compassion instills within me the knowledge that I am here on earth to do my part to help alleviate the pain of others if possible. I believe we all have the responsibility to do what we can in this regard by using our soul's unique calling towards that end.

If we are aware of our interconnectedness with others, we know that if one living being suffers, all others suffer, even if that is not readily apparent. This is because of our collective consciousness where all, including animals, are one through Spirit. Because of this unity, extending compassion on a personal level elevates the entirety of consciousness, thus propelling the collective spiritual consciousness of humanity.

In various readings I've given, as I've been detailing here, spirit beings express compassion towards family members and friends in the physical world. These readings give further credence to the fact that those in spirit are keenly aware of our feelings. The following case study, culled from many similar readings I've given, illustrates the concern and care a woman's husband in spirit has for her following his unexpected passing.

When Beverly contacts me for an appointment, I sense urgency in her voice. She wants to make a connection with someone she desperately misses and asks how soon she can come for a session. We agree upon a date and time several weeks out, though she is disappointed that it's not sooner. I sense this is because she's emotionally distraught and seeking relief but at that time, it was the soonest I could see her.

On the day of the reading, I welcome Beverly—attractive, physically fit and in her late forties—to my office. After settling in, she announces that she wants to hear from only one spirit but doesn't mention who this is. I explain how I receive the information and that there may be other spirits who want to communicate with her. I advise her to be open to whoever comes through.

From the start, I perceive a casually dressed man in shorts and a tank top standing directly beside Beverly. He wears a pleasant smile and gives me impressions about how he passed quickly from a heart attack. Because of the nature of his passing, he tells me he regrets not being able to say goodbye to her. Further, he comes through with memories he shared with Beverly like travel, boating and hiking. He shows me scenes of a beach where the couple vacationed. I relay all of this to her. She excitedly confirms this is her husband, Gary. He had passed suddenly at home when she was at work. She also confirms that she has been especially lost due to Gary's unexpected passing.

As Beverly speaks, I maintain my focus on Gary by mentally asking him what he wants to communicate to his wife. He impresses me with emotions through clairsentience.

"Gary wants to tell you he knows exactly how overwhelmed you've been since his death in the last year or so. He says his passing bowled you over emotionally because of its suddenness. You walk around in a fog and have trouble sleeping most nights. Would you agree with that?"

This message brings Beverly to tears. After a moment or so, she responds. "Yes, it's true. I don't want to go on without him. He was everything to me and now he's gone. His death happened so quickly. I lie awake most nights thinking about him, wondering if he hears me. I'm not suicidal but I don't want to be here anymore. No one seems to understand how much I miss him. I hurt so badly that ..."

Unable to finish, her voice trails off as she's overcome by emotion.

"Gary wants you to know he understands how difficult this has been for you. He knows how lonely and boxed in you've felt. He says he's been inspiring you to begin to move forward by coming out of the darkness of grief. You've been stuck in it for a long while and going in circles. He's been coming to you with this message long before this reading but because of the heaviness of grief, you haven't been open to hearing him. It's time now to go on with your life, he says."

I pause and look at Beverly. She's listening but I don't know if she really comprehends how distressing her grief is to her deceased husband. Spirits feel our pain and want us to know they are still a part of our lives. Some express that they understand our grief but that they don't want us to remain trapped within it. Obviously, Gary's aware of her emotional state and reaches out in compassion to the woman he loves. I explain that Gary's continued loving connection with his wife prompts him to offer her help.

"It's good to know Gary is okay. I mean, well, you just don't know where someone has gone who passes that quickly," Beverly says as she dabs a tissue under each eye. "I've worried that maybe he was stuck in between worlds or something. You know, I hear all sorts of things on TV shows about the afterlife. Is there anything else he wants me to know?"

"Yes. You see, it's troubling to him that you're stuck in grief. Because of his love for you, he finds it difficult to move on in the spirit world. He wants to make sure you know he'll always be with you, that this is just a temporary separation. He has work to do in spirit, but he cannot do that until he knows you are okay. Your grief is troubling to him. Oh and please don't believe everything you see on those TV shows. It's not always accurate."

Beverly nods. "I know he *must* hear me. I feel his love around me. Or am I making that up?"

"No! It's called clairsentience when we feel the presence of loved ones," I explain. "It is quite natural for us to sense their emotions and love for us. Gary says you've turned down invitations from friends to go out. He's inspired your friends to reach out to you to help. Please accept these opportunities to move forward."

"Okay, Gary, I will," Beverly promises as she gazes upward. "I just hadn't felt like going out."

"He urges you to volunteer. Get involved in helping others. When we do that, it helps us also."

"A local organization called me yesterday to see if I could give a few hours a week. Wow! I can't believe he knows that!"

"Oh, and one more thing," I say. "He wants to tell you he's going to help you with your finances since you've been overwhelmed with doing that. He wants you to call the financial advisor whose business card he had in his wallet. He's still being your husband in spirit by helping you with practical matters."

"I found that card just yesterday! There's absolutely no way you would have known about that!" she says to me with astonishment.

"Yes, but *he* knows about it and he is certainly around you. Please take his advice to live your life again. By doing so, you will honor his life. In fact, living our lives fully is the best way to honor loved ones who want the best for us."

After the session, I notice how much more relaxed Beverly appears after hearing from her late husband, a striking contrast from her solemn, anxious demeanor a mere hour earlier. She smiles and laughs while saying goodbye to me. Gary's messages of compassion for his suffering wife helped ease her broken heart and hopefully, both of them could now move forward. It was indeed a new day.

Service: The Soul's Contribution to the World

In countless readings, spirit beings deliver messages about specific services that they've offered throughout their lives. They share references about their service to church, community, schools and animal organizations, scholarships established in their memory and fundraising events such as helping raise money to pay for others' medical expenses. Once in spirit, souls realize how these contributions affect others. It's what my spirit guides have called the **ripple effect**. Just as a pebble tossed into water creates concentric ripples, a single soul's actions affect many others throughout their lives and into future generations. In turn, those souls affect others, and so on, into eternity.

The symbol of the spiral, which flows upwards and outwards, is a fitting depiction of this concept. No action is insignificant; everyone has an impact in some way. This is also illustrated in the concept of the "butterfly effect", the scientific theory that a single occurrence, no matter how small, can change the course of the universe forever. Although it's difficult (if not impossible) to know the far-reaching implications of a single act, it nonetheless leaves its imprint on others.

From what I have learned during readings, even though we may not be fully capable of understanding the far-reaching effects of our service while we are in the physical world, the interconnectedness of our impact becomes evident to us after death. In various family readings I've given, parents and ancestors come through and refer to the service they gave, its spiritual value and how it impacted others. These messages support and encourage sitters to offer their own service in life. They are a convincing validation of the remarkable value of serving interests outside of one's own.

An expression that I heard long ago has stuck with me: "Service is its own reward." As the law of karma promises, we are assured that what we give to others we also receive. Besides love, giving to others without expectation of return is one of the greatest contributions we offer the world. The form it takes doesn't matter. It's the intent behind it that does.

Giving selflessly leads us directly into the interior terrain of soul. Service amplifies and expands our connection to Spirit. When we serve, we feel our unity with all of life. False ideas of separation and superiority are obliterated when we give with an open heart. Service evolves from an earnest desire to offer our unique talents and skills to help others, improve the quality of their lives and reduce suffering in the world.

Service may or may not include monetary compensation, depending on the circumstances. One thing is certain: if we focus on what we can give to others (as opposed to our own personal gain), we draw abundance to us through the law of attraction. This is true even if we are not being compensated for our service. Interestingly, maintaining focus on serving others' needs increases what we ourselves receive—whatever form that may take. In my observation, genuinely successful people think of others first. Service that comes from the heart multiplies in concentric waves of positive energy that reaches many.

The following reading is one of dozens I've given in which the value of family and service were "topics of conversation." When families gather for readings, the bond of love they share strengthens the communication from the spirit world as the reunion takes place.

On a chilly fall evening several years ago, I drive to Pittsburgh on a "house call" to see Angela and her four siblings for a group reading at their family homestead in the city. As I approach the front door, I hear lively chatter and laughter emanating from the old brick building. Angela greets me warmly, invites me in and promptly introduces me to her brothers and sisters—Vincent, Michael, Rosalie and Anna—all gathered in the small, cozy living room. I instantly feel at ease and welcomed by this close-knit Italian family. Even though I haven't yet tuned in through mediumship, I sense there are other deceased family members in the room who are patiently waiting for the opportunity to speak. My legs and arms suddenly begin to tingle, a sure sign that Spirit is ready to communicate. As I settle into a comfortable armchair, the siblings become quiet in anticipation of what's to come. Angela sets her cell phone to record the session.

"Mom is coming through first," I begin. "She's a short, pretty woman with a smooth complexion and dark, black hair. She says she's appointed herself as the main speaker here tonight."

I'm startled by a loud burst of laughter from the group. I have no idea what I said that was so funny. Angela notices my surprise and quickly explains why the seemingly innocent message from her mother is humorous.

"My mother was the family matriarch and always appointed herself as being in charge," she says. "We never argued with her. We just accepted that. So did our dad. It's different from most Italian families where men are the head of the household, I know. But this is how we grew up. She was a strong lady."

I tune in to continue the communication. "She says one of you has part of her name. I hear 'Rose' in my mind. That must be you," I say, turning to Rosalie.

"Yes, I'm the oldest girl and Mom insisted that I be named after her. At least that's what Dad told me. Her name is Rose so she made mine a little different from hers. Dad never argued with her so that name stuck."

The communication from this assertive matriarch flows smoothly and effortlessly. I distinctly feel her strong, bold personality.

"Your mother shows me that she spent many hours sewing blankets to donate to her church and homeless shelters," I continue. "This brought her much satisfaction, she says."

"Yes, she did that for years," Rosalie confirms. "She told us it was her way of giving back for blessings received. Some of the blankets were given to sick people from our church congregation in those days. People still thank me for her contributions."

"Now she is leading me through clairvoyance into a kitchen. There are large pots of soups and sauces. I get the impression that she also cooked for others. I'm relieved that I ate before coming here tonight. This reading is making me hungry," I joke.

"Our mother made stews, soups and homemade spaghetti sauce and shared it with our neighbors," Anna says. "She always said she couldn't cook in small batches because she liked to share. Gosh, I miss her homemade sauce and meatballs!"

I silently ask Rose if there is anyone else with her who would like to speak. A few seconds lapse before I feel a male presence step in. He is waving the American flag, indicating that he was a veteran. He feels like the siblings' father. He then appears with both hands on Vincent's shoulders, a symbolic gesture of paternity. He shows me the number "one" in regard to Vincent. I'm not certain what this implies until I relay this information to him.

"I'm the oldest boy," Vincent informs me proudly. "Dad told

me to look after the family before he passed. Yes, Dad was a veteran of World War II."

"Do you recall that he told stories about his service?" I ask. "He says that he did this because he wanted people to know that he felt it was his duty to serve his country—something that brought him fulfillment. He is happy one of you has his military pins preserved in a glass case." I pause as the man imparts other impressions. "He adds that he helped other veterans in his later years. He says that he was honored to help others who were wounded in that war. This was very important to him."

"I have those pins!" Michael exclaims. "I know they meant a lot to my dad so I keep them in a special glass case. Yeah, I've heard some of Dad's stories. He loved to tell them, even though we had heard them many times. He was active in our local American Legion and marched in parades."

The reading progresses with other relatives being acknowledged, including a great-grandmother who speaks only Italian and a great-uncle who ran a tailoring shop. As the communication winds down, I see the siblings' parents step forward again. *Do they have a final message for their children?* I tune in to receive it.

"Your parents came here tonight because they know you think of them often. They also know that you pray for them and they return that to you. They leave you with the message that what they took with them to spirit was the service they gave to others during their lives. I see a red circle around this message for emphasis. Their legacy was one of service and they encourage each of you to carry it forward. This is what they want to leave you with."

I glance at the group. Angela wipes away a tear rolling down her cheek. Rosalie, too, appears to be touched by her parents' messages. The two brothers smile and nod in appreciation of their parents' parting words.

"You have no idea how spot-on that message is," Michael

pipes up. "Our parents always told us that besides their family, what they gave to others is how they want to be remembered. Please tell them we said thanks, will you?" he asks me.

"They say you've told them that many times through your thoughts," I reply. "They hear you. The love you share will never be destroyed. Neither will the service they gave."

One of the most important lessons I've learned from my connection with the spirit world is that no one is insignificant. Each soul has worth. No soul is ever lost, doomed or forgotten. There is no hierarchy of souls where some are more important than others. This is radically opposed to our earthly mindset where all too often people measure their own or others' worth by how much money they make, the possessions they own, their level of education or their physical appearances.

The spiritual truth is that all living beings are equally valuable and necessary in the unfolding divine plan. We lose sight of this when we compare ourselves to others, believe we have nothing to offer or are ashamed of who we are. Nothing we give from the heart is ever forgotten, even if we can't see it at the time.

As those in spirit confirm, all acts of kindness, compassion, gratitude and generosity matter in the glorious scheme of our spiritual evolution. Our personal contributions are noble, worthy and an essential part of the bounty of Spirit. These are the values that we take home to the spirit world and that fortify our identity as spiritual beings.

Seven. Our Wounds Do Not Dim the Light Within

The soul would have no rainbow if the eyes had no tears.
~ Native American proverb

"Do you give negative messages in readings?"

When a woman interested in having a session years ago asked me this, I wasn't sure what she meant. Her response to my request for clarification was something like, "Well you know, information that stirs up fear or is hard for people to hear."

In short, the answer is yes, I do deliver these types of messages from spirit beings. Why is it necessary that they be delivered? The fact is that these communications are only "negative" if they fall on deaf ears. Here's why:

Because readings are communications from real human beings who've experienced challenges, hardships and problems in life, not all messages are pleasant, upbeat and happy. In fact, some are downright painful for sitters to receive. However, these types of messages serve the spiritual purpose of bringing awareness to the necessity of healing these challenges and problems which often still exist in sitters' and their families' lives. Such is the case with the difficult lessons discussed in this chapter.

In all the years I've practiced mediumship, I've come to understand that direct, truthful messages play a crucial role in both sitters' and communicating spirits' spiritual healing. This is why I frequently inform people before readings that I do not censor any information that comes through. If I did, significant evidence about spirit communicators' lives may be missed and windows of opportunities to heal may not open. It is not up to me to determine what should or should not be said in readings; my job is to simply relate, as best I can, what is being communicated through me from the spirit world. If people do not want to hear the highest truth, they need to rethink having a reading with me. In the interest of helping people, I cannot sugarcoat the information. This forthrightness also serves in breaking through the denial and enforced silence of family members that are hallmarks of addictive and abusive patterns and other harmful issues.

To move beyond difficult circumstances in life, we must honestly confront issues head-on. This is true on the physical plane and also in the spirit world. If this is not done, we will be forced to repeat the lessons inherent in these situations, which gets harder each time we have that experience. This is due to the compounding of karma from earlier lessons that were unresolved. To state this another way, lessons intensify in terms of their effect on us the longer we avoid confronting them. This brings to mind the axiom, "What we resist, persists." A refusal to deal with issues, especially on the material plane, passes the unresolved issue to future generations who must then deal with it. This is in addition to communicating spirits' need to acknowledge these issues themselves in the spirit world. One way or another, unresolved and destructive patterns must be dealt with now or later, on earth or in spirit. It is much easier to handle these challenging patterns on earth because it offers teaching tools—the physical body and duality—that do not exist in spirit.

Spirit beings often refer to dealing with harmful patterns after death in order to move beyond them. In my previous books, I have written about souls having after-death counseling with specially trained spirit helpers, something I have seen through multiple sessions. This aids in the integration and assessment of the lessons spirits chose for their previous incarnations. During this process, souls gain a thorough perspective of the impact their lives and deaths had on others. This is why messages regarding the consequences of engaging in harmful behaviors are a high priority in some readings. The intent of this communication is to break the chain of the painful patterns that still exist.

If you have lost a loved one to addiction, have suffered from abuse or endured emotional or physical abandonment, I hope that you will find comfort, inspiration and encouragement in the following examples from actual readings.

A Modern Epidemic

As I write this, opioid addiction is at a record high in the United States and other nations. The latest statistics from the Centers for Disease Control show that opioid overdoses currently take the lives of more people than car accidents. Every time I watch the news or read the newspaper, there is mention of someone overdosing or dying from heroin and the powerful synthetic drug Fentanyl. According to the National Institute on Drug Abuse, young people between the ages of 18 and 25 are the likeliest group to succumb to heroin addiction, often as a result of prior synthetic opioid dependency. The lives of thousands of individuals and families are ravaged, destroyed and lost due to this epidemic. In my practice, I am reading for more families and friends than ever before who have lost loved ones from opioid addiction. It is truly heart-wrenching to witness firsthand the enormous devastation these deaths wreak on those left to cope with them.

Many individuals come to readings seeking answers to questions about deceased loved ones that they hope will bring closure to these tragic deaths. In my experience, there is no such thing as closure in untimely deaths because most people never truly "get over" losing a child, sibling, spouse or parent through unnatural circumstances. Much like losing someone to suicide or murder, substance abuse deaths defy our expectations about the natural progression of life. This is especially true in cases involving young adults. From the outside, it may appear that they are young and have everything to live for, yet inside, they are dying mentally, emotionally and physically. In most people's perception, addiction-related deaths make no sense because they seem preventable. But as you will see later in this chapter, these tragic examples are capable of being springboards for tremendous awareness and healing for other addicts and their families.

Opioids are not the only substances that destroy lives. I've heard equally horrific stories from those who've had alcoholic parents, children and other relatives. It does not matter what the substance is because all are capable of bringing the same pain and loss to addicts and their loved ones. Hearing from spirits who have passed as a direct result of addiction is a powerful testament to the deleterious consequences of it. On many occasions, it's the first time sitters become aware of their loved ones' innermost thoughts and feelings since they are commonly suppressed due to substance abuse. Through these revelations and more, the sessions help to alleviate grief by offering insights into the heart, mind and soul of the lost loved one who was shut off from them for months or years.

The next excerpt is from a session I did for the family of Clarissa, in her mid-thirties, who took her own life through a Fentanyl overdose (which was revealed through the reading).

I drive to a nearby town where Clarissa's parents reside. Upon arrival, Jilly (Clarissa's older sister) welcomes me and ushers me into the family room. There I meet Amy (Clarissa's younger sister) and their mother, Ellen. They greet me warmly and remind me that I had read for them years ago, although I don't recall any details of that.

Upon tuning into the energy around the family, I'm aware of an older woman with light-colored hair holding a cane. She impresses on me that her knees and back are painful and identifies herself as Ellen's mother. She gives several validations about her life, which the group promptly acknowledges. I perceive her with her hands placed on Ellen's right shoulder as she communicates to the family that she has a much younger woman with her. As this younger spirit steps forward, I sense her warm, bubbly and engaging personality.

"That sure sounds like Clarissa, my daughter!" Ellen exclaims. "People always said she lit up the room."

"I'm taking care of 'Issa', your mother says. Was that her nickname?" I ask them.

"Yes," Jilly answers. "My grandma called her that when she was a little girl. The name stuck and we'd also call her that sometimes."

The spirit continues to impress me with her personality (lively, quirky, curious and playful before her addiction) and various emotions she wants to convey. Clarissa also provides specific evidential messages about her relationships with each family member, which Ellen and her daughters validate. One of these messages refers to "Nancy", her nickname for Jilly who is astonished when this detail comes through. Then the reading takes on a much more serious tone.

"She says she had many ups and downs with addiction," I relay. "There were stints in rehab to get clean then she fell back into it. She uses my symbol of a merry-go-round, which means she was going in circles with this thing. She couldn't see her way clear to make a lasting change. By the way, she tells me she died from the powerful drug Fentanyl. She purposely took too much because she wanted to be out of the depression she was in. She left her body quickly. I'm sorry you have to hear this but it is the truth," I say.

Jilly confirms that her sister had gone to numerous rehab facilities but resumed drug use soon after each visit. She simply couldn't stay clean. This led to desperation and depression. The family offered help, but ultimately there was nothing they could do to stop Clarissa from making the choices she did.

"We didn't want to give up on her but each time we tried to help, she would go out and use again," Ellen says between sobs. "She had talked of ending her life. And yes, an overdose of Fentanyl was what killed her."

"Jilly, she wants to speak to you directly now," I say. "You never gave up on her, she says. You were always there for her when most people had turned their backs. For that, she thanks you. But there is an important message she wants you to know now. The last time you spoke to her, you could not have known what she was going to do. She says you've had guilt over that last phone call the two of you had, the one where you cut her off because you no longer wanted to lend her money which you knew was for drugs. That call wasn't the cause of her taking her life, not at all. *She* made that decision, not you. This all could have been prevented if she would have stayed off the drugs. But she chose not to."

"Yes, we all knew the stuff really had a hold on her," Jilly confirms. "None of us could talk her out of it. We're confused as to why she got into this in the first place. As you told us, Clarissa was full of life, outgoing and smart. It just doesn't make any sense and that makes it harder for us to accept her death."

"She says she started using drugs because inside she did not feel good about herself. Another message she's communicating is that she needed to feel accepted by others. Also, she refers to a boyfriend who used drugs. He would bring them to her. That relationship was not the best, she says. There was pressure from him to continue using."

"Oh, yes, we all know that's the truth!" exclaims Ellen. "We tried to tell her how toxic he was for her but she stayed with him. There was nothing we could say or do to convince her. In a way, I blame him for her death," she says, wiping tears from her face. "We all felt so helpless, watching her kill herself with that stuff. But what could we have done? I'm so angry at her!"

"It's understandable to feel that way, but it was Clarissa who made the choice to continue to use. She impresses me strongly that she wants you to know that she accepts responsibility for all of it. And please know she understands your feelings and is sorry to be the cause of your grief. You see, she was in so much emotional pain and depression from the drug use that she wasn't thinking clearly. Now she sees the devastation this has brought to you."

"How do we go on after this?" Amy wants to know. "A piece of our heart is missing. What can we do now?"

"First of all, she begs for your forgiveness. She is now aware of the wrong choices she made and how much they hurt her family. She was trapped in the cycle of addiction which prevented her from seeing the truth. Also, Clarissa wants you to share her story with others who have lost family members to addiction. She says she will bring others like this onto your path. Talk to them because you know the path since you have walked it. It's hard to see this now but there can be some good that will come from this. As you help others in similar situations, you will help yourselves."

With this message, the reading draws to a close. Ellen, Jilly and Amy hug me and offer their thanks. As I drive home, I think about the family and the impact Clarissa's messages likely had on them. I say a little prayer that the reading offers them comfort and serves as a turning point for them to move beyond pain and into understanding and forgiveness.

Clarissa's final message about sharing her story of addiction and suicide with other families is one that I've heard from others who have passed in the same manner. Despite their devastating loss, this family could eventually support and inspire others in the same unfortunate situation. Anger, guilt, confusion and grief weigh heavily on those who lose someone dear to addiction. Letting go of these burdens brings peace and acceptance. Although life will never be the same for families who have had tragic deaths such as Clarissa's, there is life, peace and comfort available through the endless, ever-present love of Spirit. Nothing can ever separate us from that source of infinite love.

Abuse, Abandonment and Self-Worth

For most people, parents are their primary source of love, nurturing and caregiving from birth into adulthood. When I was growing up during the 1960s and early '70s, I was blessed to have two loving parents whom I could always count on to feed, house and clothe me. I went to bed each night feeling safe, secure and loved. It was not until my junior high years, when I interacted with other classmates, that I realized not everyone had the same happy home life that I enjoyed.

One day, a girl I became close friends with in seventh grade confided in me that her uncle was sexually abusing her. Needless to say, I was horrified. I had no idea how to react to her confession. In my sheltered life, I had never heard of this type of behavior since it was long before sexual abuse was openly discussed on TV, the news or in "polite conversation." Each day in English class, this friend wrote me candid notes about how her uncle had initiated sex with her the evening before. In addition, she admitted that she liked the attention and wanted it to continue because (in her estimation) it made her feel loved. I kept her confession to myself even though I intuitively knew what she was experiencing was wrong. It never occurred to me to report this to the school nurse or anyone else since sexual abuse was not normally acknowledged in those days.

When I finally gained some sense about the matter and intuitively realized that this was wrong, I told her she needed to tell her parents about it. Her response was that they would not believe her. On top of that, she thought sex was a measure of the love her uncle felt for her. That was the end of the story and the notes. She dropped the topic and never brought it up again, although we remained friends for the rest of the school year. This incident was one of the first times that I became aware that some kids came from families that radically differed from mine.

Although abuse takes various forms, there is one central theme that runs through it: the degradation of a living being by another who inflicts power and control. It often occurs in cycles, starting with the escalating anger and exploitation of power by the perpetrator, the abuse itself, the quieting-down phase (sometimes called the "honeymoon" phase) and then back again to the escalation phase. Until the one who suffers from abuse decides enough is enough, the destructive cycle continues, producing physical, emotional and mental wounds that impact a person's entire life. In some cases, abuse results in death for one or both parties.

In my work, I have heard abuse in families mentioned by spirit communicators and sitters multiple times. In my opinion, it is one of the most difficult patterns to cope with since it is hidden from others (especially in the case with sexual abuse), not openly discussed among family members or repressed within one's own subconscious mind. Many people feel deep shame about having these harrowing experiences and so decline to share them with others. Recovering from abuse involves meeting it head-on, openly and honestly, without shame. In some cases, this means the entire family of the abused person must emerge from denial to face the devastating effects the behavior has had upon them and possibly previous generations.

In the following reading, the communicating spirit delivers messages about abuse from his father and its consequences on his life. It illustrates how the crisis of suicide and the revelation of long-kept secrets can serve as catalysts for an entire family's growth and awakening. It also contains an unexpected message about reconciliation.

Margie and her two children, John and Jackie, call my office for a phone reading. During my opening prayer, I become aware of a short, muscular man wearing jeans and sporting a beard. He is standing next to Margie. He impresses on me that he'd died within the past year. Further, he gives me the feeling of fuzziness in his head, a sensation that spirits use to indicate that they used drugs or alcohol. I relate this to the family.

Margie is the first to respond. "That sounds like Paul, my husband. He always wore jeans and was short and muscular. He lifted weights at the gym. We had no idea he was drinking as much as he was until after his death when we found lots of hidden whiskey bottles in the basement."

"He makes me feel that he took himself out by committing suicide," I say. "I also get the feeling something was skewed with his thinking. It was up and down. A mental illness, perhaps?" I ask.

"Yes, he had bipolar disorder and he took his own life with a gun," Jackie replies.

At this point, I become aware that the link between Paul and me is weak. It feels as if the communication is strained and difficult, like pulling teeth to get information from him. *What could this mean?* I pass this observation along to the family.

"Oh, that makes perfect sense!" Margie says. "He kept everything buried, his feelings, I mean. He didn't discuss them with any of us. He kept everything to himself. It was very frustrating. If we would have known how badly he felt, well, maybe we could have gotten him help."

So that explains the difficult communication between us. It was a blank feeling, as if no emotions were present. This made sense since this man didn't express himself in life. I send him a beam of love in hopes that he will connect more deeply with us.

"No wonder this feels strange," I comment. "He is not forthcoming at all now because that's the way he was in life. He gives me the impression that he suppressed bad memories from his childhood. It's hard for him to talk about these." I send thoughts to the man, asking him to give me more information about this part of his life. I assure him that this will help both him and his family. I close my eyes to focus on the subtle impressions. Finally, a breakthrough comes.

"There was terrible emotional and physical abuse from his

dad, he says. His father was cruel to him, and because of that, he never felt good about himself. He felt worthless and that is why he drank so much. He also tells me he thought about suicide other times during his life. He didn't trust anyone and that's why he kept everything to himself."

"Oh, yes! I knew about the abuse from his father, even though he never fully opened up about it," Margie confirms. "He had nothing to do with his father for years before the old man passed over so I knew their relationship must have been bad. He wouldn't even mention his name!"

Next, Paul shows me handwritten letters, which I describe to the family.

This time, it's John, his son, who validates. "Yep, we found those letters after his death. They were former suicide notes. We don't know why he kept those around. My father had such a hard time in life. He refused to talk about the way his dad treated him but we knew it was something he wasn't able to get over."

Suddenly, I hear the name "Keith" through clairaudience.

"Oh, my!" Margie exclaims on the other end of the phone. "I can hardly believe it! Keith is my husband's son who called us shortly after Paul passed. We never knew he existed before that. Does this mean Paul knows we are going to meet Keith over the holidays?"

"Yes, he does know. He is the one who inspired Keith to contact you after his death. You see, once he was in spirit, he realized that he needed to divulge all of the secrets he kept from you. He says he saw that he withheld so much out of shame and false pride, that it hurt you and the family. He also inspired you where to find those handwritten suicide notes. By reading these, you could understand his feelings better."

After several other messages from Paul, which Margie validates, he shows me an image of himself standing with his arm around an older man by his side. This image comes with a message from Paul—one that I sense might be difficult for the family to comprehend.

"Paul shows me that he and his dad have reconciled in spirit. They appear together with Paul's arm around him. They are not only together, he says, but he adds that they have forgiven the past. Both knew they had to do this in order to accelerate their spiritual growth. Once in spirit, Paul saw that his relationship with his dad was one he chose to develop qualities of inner strength and self-reliance in addition to learning how to forgive. He didn't do well on earth with this lesson because he tried to drown his feelings with alcohol. His father could have chosen to present this lesson in a better way but he failed. But Paul has now forgiven his father for the abuse."

The family is silent on the other end of the phone. I sense they are shocked by this. Jackie finally speaks up.

"What does this all mean for us left behind? I mean, what are we to do with that information? It was really my grandfather's fault that Dad was so messed up!"

To help them understand, I knew I had to give the family an explanation about difficult lessons in life from a spiritual perspective. "In a way, yes it was, but in reality, your dad made the choice to remain a victim of his father's abuse long past his childhood. He chose to become a prisoner of it instead of learning and growing from it. This doesn't mean he's a bad person but that he will now have to progress from that point in the spirit world since he ended his physical life. Your family's lesson here is to first understand the pattern of abuse and then release it so it's not repeated. Share your feelings with each other honestly and openly. Much time has passed with feelings being neglected. You must talk about this and other important matters to break the old patterns of secrecy and shame. He urges you to do this."

"I suppose he's right," Margie says with a sigh. "It's very hard, though. I have so many feelings to get over. It's difficult for me to share these because I'm so confused about them. I feel as if I never really knew my husband, even though we'd been together for over 25 years. He was so secretive."

"One last message comes through," I say. "Paul wants each of you to live your lives better than he did. He's going to stay around to help you. By being open with one another, you will grow closer, live your lives to the fullest and honor his life instead of carrying the pain of it. Please think about that."

Abandonment

In addition to abuse, the reading with Paul's family addresses the topic of abandonment, the loss or absence of close, nurturing relationships, usually early in one's life. In this case, Paul's father abandoned him emotionally from the time he was a young child. Abandonment occurs in families where one or both parents have passed, parents are unable or unwilling to care for children due to addiction or illness, or they divorce when children are young. It's also the case that if parents did not receive love from their parents, they sometimes lack the capacity to give it to their children. If parents were around physically but addicted, they were not emotionally or mentally capable of meeting the needs of their children. When any of these circumstances happen, children experience a range of troubling emotions like confusion, grief, loneliness, anger and depression. They may also feel responsible for driving their parents away during a divorce or assume they are accountable for a parent's death, drug addiction or alcoholism. In the case of divorce or addiction, they may unconsciously internalize the pain of one or both parents out of loyalty.

Every human being seeks physical and emotional nurturing and love. In families where these basic needs are not met, children attempt to obtain them through unconsciously "volunteering" to carry the trauma of emotionally wounded parents. To obtain the love they crave, these children display loyalty to be the "good" girl or boy to alleviate their parents' pain. In doing so, they believe that they will finally obtain the love they desperately need. In addition, they may wrongly assume there is something inherently wrong with them that caused a parent to leave the family home, become addicted or die. If a caring adult doesn't explain the truth to them, these harmful assumptions become reality in their innocent minds.

Children do not have the reasoning capability of adults and therefore do not understand that they had nothing to do with their parents' separation, divorce or addiction. Nor do they comprehend that if people do not recognize love within themselves, they cannot give it to others. In the perspective of some children, the way to get love is to become mom or dad's best friend by vowing to take away their pain and carry it for them. Then they will be loved and rewarded for easing the pain of their parents. When that inevitably fails, children try harder to *earn* love that should be given unconditionally. This can involve attention seeking, risky behaviors, becoming the perfect child to gain approval or getting entangled in emotional incest where the boundaries between parent and child are severely distorted or nonexistent. To those who feel unloved, any of these is preferable to the misery of feeling unwanted and lonely.

When children who have experienced abandonment become adults and enter into relationships, sooner or later the issue of abandonment surfaces and causes problems. People may create emotional distance from a partner who they believe will ultimately leave them or they may become overly dependent and clingy. Having never had a healthy relationship with parents, they often have no idea how to relate well with others. Or they become like Paul in the prior reading: distrusting everyone and internalizing all feelings because of a fear of vulnerability. Also like Paul, some people may tragically take their own lives to escape feelings of abandonment, loneliness and unworthiness.

The good news is that every person who suffers from addiction, abuse or abandonment has the choice to transcend and ultimately conquer these frightening conditions through support groups, in-patient treatment facilities, psychotherapy, 12-step recovery groups, and with the help of family and friends. In my experience, people who develop a spiritual awareness during treatment are much more likely to succeed than those who don't. Without this vital anchor, it's all too easy to fall back into old ways of thinking, long-held patterns and self-sabotage.

The Higher Self as Healer of Addiction, Abuse and Abandonment

Fundamental to recovery and healing is the awareness of one's own higher self (the soul), which exists beyond the influence of addiction and feelings of self-loathing created by abuse and abandonment. From its perspective, these conditions are simply experiences; that is, there is no emotional attachment to them or judgment about them (since attachment comes from the mind), only the observation of them. From the viewpoint of the higher self, these experiences have only one purpose: to invariably lead us back home to the awareness of our authentic identity as divine beings. *There is no other purpose to suffering than the awakening to the truth of Spirit within.* This is the gift it offers us. This is also why incredibly traumatic circumstances can lead people to heights of spiritual and personal transformation.

Connecting with the higher self bypasses judgment. Why is this important to healing? Many people who are addicted, abused or have experienced childhood abandonment are self-critical because of untrue beliefs about their own self-worth. These damaging beliefs are a product of the rational mind, the seat of all judgment. As long as people remain attached to thoughts of unworthiness and shame, they will remain unhappy by attracting the same defeating circumstances and relationships. To heal these patterns, we must change the thoughts that created them. One way to do this is by becoming an observer of one's own thoughts through daily connection with the higher self, the place where self-nurturing and unconditional love reside.

The following meditation is an easy way to do that. (Note: You can do this simple exercise right now if you are sitting or lying down. It's important to release expectations about what you will experience before you begin this exercise. The point is to relax and be open.)

Sit quietly, close your eyes and focus on your breath as you inhale, hold for a few seconds and then exhale. Allow yourself to relax, beginning with your feet and moving up your body to the top of your head. With each exhalation, mentally picture stress, anxiety and any physical pain drift away from you in a bubble. If thoughts come in as you continue to breathe (and they will), simply notice them as they float in and out of your consciousness. If they are persistent, continue to observe them with curiosity. There is no reason to fear these; they arise and they move on much like clouds drifting across the sky. By detaching from them, you are using your power to observe your own thoughts. Whatever thoughts come, simply notice them without attaching judgment to them or necessarily believing them. Allow these to come and go as you continue to breathe for a moment or so.

As you continue to relax and breathe normally, place your attention and a hand on your chest—specifically, on your heart. Now think of the last time you gave or received love. (This can be anything: a relationship with a person, bonding with a beloved pet, a blessing you've recently received or an event or situation for which you are extremely grateful.) Feel your heart gently soften and open in response to your higher self's awareness of that love. Notice how your body responds to these self-affirming thoughts. Stay in this glow of love for a minute or so. In this expanded state, realize that harmony, peace, love, joy and gratitude exist at the core of your being. This is your higher self speaking directly to you through the energy of love. You are no longer controlled by the incessant thoughts and beliefs of your mind, but safely enfolded within your soul's perfect, elevated perspective. In this state, there is no judgment of self or others; there is only peace and unity.

Remember that this sanctuary is always available to you, especially those times you feel frazzled and scattered by vexing thoughts such as doubt, anxiety or fear. Now slowly open your eyes. Become aware of your feet and hands. Breathe deeply and relax. Be thankful. A new, bright day is here for you in this very moment.

The soul's awareness is a lifeline that diffuses turmoil. Think of it as a life preserver. By connecting with this higher awareness, we can overcome problems, defeat negative thinking and erase doubt by replacing them with trust, self-confidence and inner peace. To eradicate self-defeating thoughts and beliefs, it's helpful to connect with your higher self daily.

Also vital to recovery is the recognition that we are not the thoughts and experiences we *have*. They define and limit us only if we allow that to happen. Problems arise when we become lost in thoughts and experiences through *identifying* with them. The same is true when we allow the past to overshadow the present moment. Not only does the past not exist, it holds no power over our free will to make different choices today. In every minute, we have the ability to choose differently. The foundation for successful recovery from traumatic events is transforming oneself from the inside out. If internal changes don't happen, recovery will not be lasting or won't occur at all. By reaching fearlessly within ourselves to the very core of our being, we extract the rich treasures offered by the higher self: fortitude, patience, resiliency, faith and hope, among others.

The higher self thrives in the energy of freedom. Our soul yearns to experience the liberation that comes from releasing outworn thoughts, beliefs and patterns that shroud its brilliance. In fact, this is why each of us has come to the physical dimension: to reveal the untarnished perfection and beauty of our soul. Earth as a schoolroom offers us ample opportunities to evolve through myriad events. A helpful perspective to adopt is that challenging events always contain the hidden gem of greater self-awareness and evolution.

Growing up in the spiritual sense inevitably involves falling down and getting hurt again and again; but if we wholeheartedly accept that our souls come into physical reality to fearlessly experience the adventure of being human, growth becomes much easier. The thrilling odyssey of uncovering one's true self is never ending—even after we part this world.

Eight. Releasing the Past Accelerates Our Spiritual Growth

Forgiveness is my function as the light of the world.
~ *A Course in Miracles*, Lesson 62

While growing up during the 1960s, I attended Sunday school in a Protestant church where my parents were members. One of my classes was taught by Miss Hild, who was extremely knowledgeable about the Bible. During the Lenten season, we had to memorize the final seven sayings of Jesus as He hung on the cross. One of these is "Father, forgive them, for they know not what they do" [Luke 23:34].

As an 11 year old, I remember wondering how Jesus could have forgiven people who mocked, tortured and killed him. To me, such an attitude of kindness seemed impossible even for the Son of God. Also baffling was the second part of Jesus' sentence, "for they know not what they do." I couldn't fathom how anyone could not be aware of how wrong it was to commit a vile act like crucifixion. Miss Hild told us that Jesus' holiness and purity made it possible to forgive such hatred. *But did this mean we, too, were equally capable of forgiving others when they cruelly hurt us or our loved ones? Jesus was the Son of God and that made him special in terms of doing the seemingly impossible. Are we all capable of letting go of such pain?* I wondered.

Since those early days in Sunday school, I presumed that forgiveness meant to let go of anger and blame towards another who had harmed me. Several decades later, I formed a new understanding of forgiveness, which came about through my studies of the spiritual text *A Course in Miracles* (Foundation for Inner Peace, 1975). I began to see forgiveness in another light: letting go of the past—specifically the outworn thoughts, beliefs and behavior patterns that had become lodged in my mind. The

Course teaches that forgiveness is the sole function of each soul because forgiveness is the abiding presence of the Christ (the divine pattern of perfection and wholeness) present in all of us. This innate perfection of souls is what the Course refers to as "Real." It renders everything else "unreal", including sins we think we are "guilty" of. The Course teaches that it is impossible for us to be guilty of anything because we are all sons of God and are made in that divine image.

What Jesus meant by "for they know not what they do" is that He understood the consciousness present in those who killed Him. His persecutors did not have the spiritual consciousness necessary to recognize Jesus as an elevated being who had come to help humankind because they were controlled by fear, jealousy and self-centeredness. They were threatened by the prospect of leaving the familiar dictates and teachings of religion and by the inner transformation this departure would inevitably bring. Those in positions of power in the churches feared losing their authority over others—a loss that they could not tolerate. It was easier to kill the one who attempted to introduce such radical changes than to accept and follow Him. He was simply too threatening to the societal and religious structures that were in place.

These spiritual lessons helped me to get in touch with lingering issues that haunted me from the past, namely recurring thoughts of regret about my young adult years. Over time, I saw that letting go of these led me directly into my higher self, where peace resides. I realized that I had no power to change the past but I did have the ability to alter my perceptions about it. Why was I continuing to condemn myself for acting as I did back then? Should I look upon all I did in those days as "mistakes"? Or could I reframe my view of the events to perceive them as pivotal, necessary events in my personal journey of spiritual awakening? Reframing the past involves the understanding that we make decisions and take action based on the consciousness we have at that time. With this recognition and acceptance, we can forgive both ourselves and others.

In my case, guilt and regret seemed to serve no purpose except to make me miserable. Over time, I realized that if I had known better in those days, I would have made much different choices. I decided to let guilt and regrets go. The journey of self-forgiveness renews daily as I cleanse old thoughts and beliefs from my mind to avoid accumulation of that debris. This newfound practice of forgiveness has been one of the most profound, central lessons in my life.

Genuine forgiveness is making a conscious choice to release the encumbrance of the past, which dwells in the thinking mind and perceives the past as real. But the past no longer exists except in the mental constructs of memories. The same is true of the future, which is nothing more than thoughts conjured by the mind. In reality, each of us has only the present moment at our disposal. This is where forgiveness resides: in each moment. It is a conscious decision to let go of grievances like anger, resentment and revenge that we carry in our mental narrative about perceived wrongdoings of our own or those perpetrated on us. Continuing to hold onto these emotional toxins attracts similar negative feelings, circumstances and events in a self-perpetuating cycle.

Our natural inclination is to feel justified in holding onto these emotions because of the pain we acquired from the situation. Blaming others is far easier than accepting responsibility for our own reactions to a situation because then we must emerge from our comfort zone and confront the need to change. In an energetic sense, holding onto guilt, anger, hatred and resentment binds us negatively to the situation and the people involved with it. This creates and sustains karmic ties with these souls and delays our own growth. In the case of self-blame, clinging to these emotions fosters guilt and self-deprecation. Cleansing these lower thoughts and emotions detoxifies the mind, even if those who have hurt us are unapologetic. This is what my spirit guides call "keeping your slate clean", something they have gently reminded me of through the years. As stated earlier, issues that are not addressed on the physical plane will need to be dealt with in the spirit world. In various readings, spirit beings have repeatedly expressed this truth, along with regrets for not having done the work sooner.

Each person has the ability to move beyond the past by engaging in forgiveness. Even if a grievance has been held for many years, it can be dropped in an instant with the intent to be free of it. Forgiveness ushers in freedom because it releases us from the bondage of anger, resentment, sadness and hatred. The ultimate reward is inner peace.

I once heard someone remark that if we could approach our spouse each day as if we were meeting him or her for the first time — innocently, open-mindedly and without an agenda — we would not harbor resentments that fuel arguments. If we used this same approach with *all* relationships, the world would be very different. There would be no basis for conflicts, disagreements or wars. In order to accomplish this, we need to bypass the rational mind's misperceptions of judgment concerning others. This is not an easy task but one that certainly offers the noble gifts of understanding, compassion, peace, honest communication and cooperation where everyone benefits.

Self-Forgiveness is Core to Healing

The famous artist Salvador Dalí once said, "Have no fear of perfection; you'll never reach it." As students in earth's classroom, we will experience failure as we go about the business of living. Many times, we fall short of our greatest potential. To expect otherwise is to live in naïveté and a false sense of perfectionism. Shortcomings are opportunities in disguise. They provide clarity about what we value, how we can improve and insights about right direction according to our soul's divine purpose. One of the greatest assets we own is the ability to change. Personally, I do not believe the old axioms, "A leopard never changes its spots" or "You can't teach an old dog new tricks." We have the ability to change anything about ourselves at any time if we possess the sincere intent to do so.

In my journey of self-forgiveness concerning the wild days of my early adulthood, one of the issues I wrestled with was forgiving myself for the callous manner in which I treated my parents and others. I lived with reckless abandon and little regard for the feelings of others. I had a self-centered perspective. So when those old memories troubled me years later, it didn't matter that I had been free from alcohol for decades and currently lived a spiritually centered life. The old memories of my harsh treatment of others continued to play out relentlessly in my mind.

During this time, I had returned to traditional religion and began attending a local Protestant church weekly. Each service included the forgiveness of sins through the blessing of the redemption of Christ. Over the course of many months, I came to understand that by carrying the damaging mindset of not forgiving myself, I was harming myself further by remaining bound to a past that I was powerless to change. How could I possibly be available to live life in joy, purpose and peace in present time? By all accounts, I was not the same person now as then. The realization came to me that if I would have *known* better in those days, I would have acted better. If I would have had more spiritual awareness and less self-centeredness, I would have treated others with much more care, kindness and compassion. This new perspective enabled me to move beyond the self-punishing guilt. I also made countless amends to my mother in spirit for my treatment of her. I know she has forgiven me, as she's come to me and said so.

I'm aware that I'm not alone in undertaking the challenging work of self-forgiveness. I've met others who struggle with this same issue. I have given readings to people who admit having no problem forgiving others but find it daunting to let go of their own past mistakes, failures and wrongdoings. Interestingly, some of these acts are not "wrong" at all, just misperceptions. In other words, people hold themselves to an unrealistic standard of behavior and then feel guilt when they come up short. This is especially true regarding relationships with deceased loved ones where regrets may linger.

Many people entertain thoughts that they "should" or "could" have done something differently, but now it's too late to make changes because the person they believe they hurt has died. In some cases, people carry unnecessary guilt, remorse or self-blame for years over past relationships by berating themselves endlessly or adhering to perfectionism. An example of this is when a person has guilt over not being present when a loved one dies.

I once did a reading for a woman who sat with her husband day after day while he was dying from cancer. One day, she left the room to get lunch and when she returned, he had passed. During the reading, he emphasized that he went when he did because it was his soul's time to do so. He also mentioned the names of relatives who received him in spirit. Although his wife had imagined her taking lunch at the moment of his death to be something regrettable, he verified that this had no negative influence on him whatsoever. Additionally, he mentioned that she had done her part well in helping him while he was ill. His message left a positive impression on his wife because after the session ended, she admitted feeling extremely guilty about not being been present at the moment of his passing. After hearing from him directly, however, she realized the guilt she was carrying was an invention of her mind, an untrue perception that dissolved after the session. (To read more examples of self-forgiveness and healing during readings, see my book, *Soul to Soul Connections: Comforting Messages From the Spirit World*.)

People have asked me if it's possible to communicate about forgiveness to or from those in spirit. The answer to this is a resounding yes. They know when we ask and that we desire to be free of the past. If you feel that you genuinely need to ask for forgiveness from a loved one in spirit, don't delay. Do it now to free yourself from carrying the burden. In communicating forgiveness, you will extricate both yourself and your loved one from holding any issues between you. You will feel a new lightness and a fresh beginning when you let go.

What happens in a spiritual sense when one party has forgiven but the other hasn't? What if the other person continues to hold resentments toward us? Because we are responsible for our own life only, we cannot change anyone else's attitude. Therefore, forgiveness is an act that you must do for yourself in the interest of self-purification and obtaining freedom. It's best not to concern yourself with what anyone is or isn't doing. Simply focus on yourself.

Forgiveness is the foundation of spiritual, emotional, mental and physical healing. It is absolutely essential in the evolution of the soul's journey towards the awareness of its divine spiritual identity. It is so fundamental to healing that I've come to think of it as the cornerstone of healing, the first "stone" set in the construction of a new way of being. Without it, we would collapse beneath the heaviness of layers of old thoughts, beliefs and patterns that obscure the magnificent light of our souls. Forgiveness ushers in radiant, refreshing energy to create life the way we want it to be, unencumbered by the past.

Forgiveness Releases Karma

Lower vibratory thoughts, emotions and actions that we create during physical life are blockages that inhibit our spiritual growth and prevent us from realizing the extraordinary splendor of our souls. These lower vibrations become part of our personal karma. If these become deeply entrenched by our refusal to address them, we end up trapped by these self-made illusions. Because we alone are responsible for everything we create, we will eventually have to confront, examine and release these misperceptions that are obstacles to our growth.

When the soul takes on a physical incarnation, it retains the memory of its perfection, even though the mind and personality frequently take precedence over its expression. The journey of awakening simply means that we remember that pure expression. As you have seen through the stories in earlier chapters, this often happens through some form of suffering, the so-called "dark night" described by various spiritual masters. Because the eternal light of the soul can never be extinguished, it will always be present at the center of our being. It may take years or many lifetimes to come to this realization, although the soul knows nothing of time. The higher consciousness of forgiveness is a powerful catalyst in this awakening process. In the illumination of divine awareness, dark energies are dispelled. You will move along your pathway more quickly through releasing the past.

The simplest way to forgive is by setting your intent to do so in writing. It's helpful to state this in clear, simple, specific terms. For example: *I forgive* _____ (fill in with a person or "myself") *for* _____ (fill in with the particular circumstance you are forgiving). Call upon the higher assistance of your soul to help during this exercise. Then bring to mind the person and situation. If it's you, see yourself in place of the other person. Visualize both of these surrounded by violet light (this color purifies lower energy). Hold this image for a few moments until the images dissolve in your awareness. Take a cleansing breath and affirm, "*I now release all thoughts and emotions connected to* _____ (the person and situation). *I am free of the past.*" Place your full attention on your breath. Give thanks to Spirit for this fresh start.

Should you meet with resistance about forgiving yourself or others, call upon your higher self to give you the *willingness* to forgive. This is helpful in instances where we believe the perceived offense is difficult or impossible to release. It's not necessary to have feelings of warmth or friendliness towards others involved; your willingness is enough to incline your mind in the direction of forgiveness. We may feel justified in holding onto the grudge or afraid of our own vulnerability if we let it go. Asking for the willingness to let go loosens the mind's grip on the issue. You can then proceed with the exercise of releasing it.

Each time we move beyond the past, whatever it may involve, we move closer to the divine consciousness of the soul. Each instance in which we accept life exactly as it is without the blinders of past thoughts, reactions and conditioning brings us into deeper alignment with Spirit. Every release of "what was" opens the door to "what is", the unlimited potential contained within us.

I first met Jeff and his partner, Karen, at a group reading years ago. I did not know them personally but had connected with them briefly when several of their relatives in spirit communicated through me. Years after this first meeting, I happened to be on Facebook one day and noticed a post from Karen about Jeff's daughter, Miranda, 31, who had been murdered. I purposely scrolled quickly past these posts because I intuitively felt that Jeff may call me for a session. In any case, I didn't want to know the details of his daughter's death should I be called upon to do a reading for him.

Just as I had felt, Karen e-mailed me several months later to set up a phone session for Jeff. I instructed her to tell Jeff about the customary preparations of having questions written down and to engage in meditation prior to the session.

On the day of the appointment, Jeff calls my office. At the start of the session, I explain that I know about his daughter's passing but not the circumstances surrounding it. I tell him that in cases where I know a few facts prior to a session, I ask those in spirit to "step it up a notch" by giving specific evidence that I could not or do not know. By stating this intent, the reading has more power in terms of healing.

"An older male who feels like a dad comes through first. He has several other souls with him in spirit. He impresses on me that he passed from a heart condition and also had other things wrong with his body. In fact, there were several physical issues going on with him. There's also a contemporary of your dad's (from the same generation as Jeff's father) here who says you have his first name."

"Yes, my dad had cardiac issues, kidney and spine problems," Jeff confirms. "I was named after my Uncle Jeff, Dad's brother."

Suddenly, I'm aware of a shift in the energy around me as another spirit, a female, is ushered through by Jeff's dad. She stands beneath him in my mind's eye, indicating she is younger than him. I telepathically ask this spirit to come closer so I can merge with her. I close my eyes and tune in to receive her thoughts.

"Your daughter is here, Jeff. I perceive her spirit light as very bright. This means in life she was kind, gentle and giving. She has pretty blonde hair and a big smile. She says she wants you to know she is with Grandpa and other relatives from both sides of your family. She wants you to know they are taking care of her. It was a bit difficult for her after she passed since she died so unexpectedly."

I hear Jeff break down sobbing on the other end of the phone. I tear up also but retain my composure to do the reading. A moment goes by then another message comes into my awareness from the young woman.

"She says you expressed warnings to her about the man who murdered her long ago, back when they were dating. She indicates this is her husband. She didn't want to believe these and wanted to give the marriage an honest effort. Before they married, she had doubts about him but kept those to herself. He had two sides to him. He could be very charming but also very mean-spirited and manipulative. I mention this, Jeff, because your daughter is showing me the symbol of a mask, which means a two-faced person. Also, she says people were genuinely shocked when they heard about the murder as they thought he wouldn't be capable of such an act. They knew only the charming side of your son-in-law."

"Yes, yes!" Jeff exclaims. "So many people told me that afterwards. He had all of them fooled. But I had always felt something wasn't right about him and warned her about this. He tried hard to control Miranda. She gave in to keep the peace. I believe she was afraid of him."

Jeff sobs again. I feel his deep sorrow over the loss of his daughter who died at the hands of her husband. This is another instance in which I'm aware that I have to practice emotional detachment to stay open to the communication. I take a breath and refocus on the young woman's vibrant spirit.

"Miranda has been coming to you for quite some time wanting you to know she's safe with your dad. Also, she emphasizes that she's aware that you feel guilty about this and to drop that feeling. There was nothing you could have done to prevent it."

Jeff chokes back more tears. "I feel I should have been there to protect her because she was my daughter. I'm tortured by that guilt every day since she died. Maybe if I would have done that, she would still be alive. She must know my private thoughts then."

"Yes, she surely does," I assure him. "She also says you talk to her every day and she hears you. It's time to let go of the guilt and forgive yourself for something you could not have prevented. There is no way you are responsible for what happened to her."

"Yes, I do talk to her," he replies, still crying. "It's hard to let go of the guilt. I should have known or done something ..." Jeff's voice trails off.

"You couldn't have," I assure him. "It serves no purpose now to feel guilty for something you had no control over."

As the reading progresses, Miranda shows me several significant items through clairvoyance. "There's a photo of her with a dog she says you keep out all the time. This is part of the memorial you made for her in your home. She is taking me there now, right into the room where you watch TV and spend evenings. There is an easy chair there with a lamp beside it and a colorful braided rug. She wants you to know you can connect with her in that place."

"Yes, it is in that room I've felt her!" Jeff confirms. "It is as you described it."

"There is something hanging by a string or cord that she mentions. Um, wait ... it appears to be a necklace of some sort," I say as I try to perceive more details of the object. "And then the picture transforms into something belonging to her that hangs in a car." I'm puzzled by what Miranda is attempting to communicate. "Would you understand this?" I ask him.

"It's her remains. I wear them in a necklace around my neck every day. They are on a black cord. I don't know what the other thing in the car is."

"Please check with your family and see if one of them would know," I advise.

Next, Miranda impresses me with clairvoyant scenes of a beautiful, serene lake and a boat, which I describe to Jeff.

"We used to go boating on a lake we visited many times. We loved it there."

"Yes, she is coming through with memories of your life together." I sense Miranda wants me to add more to the image of the lake through giving me feelings. I tune in to interpret these correctly.

"The quiet beauty of that lake ... Miranda wants you to know this is her way of telling you she is at peace in the spirit world. She says that when you think of her, think of her in this way, at peace and happy in a beautiful place. She says that will help you."

At this point, I feel Miranda's energy recede, signaling the close of the communication. I thank Jeff for his trust in me as a conduit and remind him of his daughter's strong message about forgiving himself from the punishing guilt he has carried.

"I can't tell you how much hearing from Miranda has helped me, Carole. It is a bright spot in the midst of the darkness of her death. Please, will you thank Miranda for talking to me?"

"She hears you," I assure him. Before hanging up I suggest to Jeff that counseling would be helpful in dealing with his guilt and grief over the death of his daughter. On my prayer list, I write his name to support him with spiritual strength during the upcoming court trial of his son-in-law. I say a small prayer of thanks for Spirit's support and assistance during the emotionally difficult reading. The grace and comfort of Spirit is always present, even in the most unfathomably painful circumstances.

In the case of guilt, it's helpful to consider the root cause(s) of why we think we're guilty. The true meaning of guilt is remorse for something we intentionally did to cause harm to another. It is our conscience telling us to make a correction to this harmful behavior. Unfortunately, many people mistakenly believe that guilt is an appropriate response to events over which they have little or no control. The difference between this faulty perception and genuine guilt lies in understanding one's responsibility (or lack thereof) for the guilt-inducing event.

To clarify, if I intentionally hurt someone, I may have genuine guilt because I am directly responsible for my words and actions that have harmed another. On the other hand, if an event happens that I am in no way responsible for, I cannot feel real guilt since I did not have a direct hand in causing that event. I may feel sadness or sorrow about the event that has occurred but if I am not responsible for causing it, I am not guilty of anything concerning it. This is an important distinction to know because it can prevent needless self-punishment from misperceptions.

If you are carrying guilt over an event that you had no responsibility in causing, release it today. If you do bear responsibility, make amends to the person(s) involved whenever possible. In either case, each act of forgiveness is a significant step forward for your soul.

Betrayal and Forgiveness

Forgiving a spouse, partner or friend who betrays us is especially challenging since the bond of trust is destroyed. Whatever form the betrayal takes—infidelity, misuse of shared money or damaging gossip—the road to healing is a long, arduous one. In some cases, people decide to end the relationship because of the betrayal. In others, the relationship must be rebuilt through dedication, honesty and sustained effort on the behalf of both parties. There's no easy, fast way to confront and cope with betrayal since it often shatters us to our core. The next excerpt is from a reading with a woman who discovered the painful truth about her husband's secret life. This situation illustrates how betrayals function as wakeup calls that are capable of leading us to higher ground in terms of personal growth.

Anne, 42, an attractive woman with shiny, long, dark hair and sparkling blue eyes, visits my office for a half-hour session. She informs me that she was referred by Mindy, the owner of a yoga studio I've visited several times to present group mediumship. As we begin, I ask if she wants to hear from loved ones in spirit.

"Yes," Anne replies with a hint of nervousness in her voice.

As I recite my prayer, I feel the familiar tingling in my legs indicating Spirit's presence. In seconds, I become aware of an older woman who stands behind and to the right of Anne.

"I have a woman here connecting with you who feels like a Mom. She impresses me that she had major health issues in her chest area and shows me my symbol for a procedure or surgery:

a scar. Her illness was a longer one and she was relieved to pass since she was so uncomfortable. She was very tired at the end. Does this make sense?"

"Yes," Anne says in a soft voice. "That's Mom. She passed from lung issues that caused heart failure. She was really tired at the end. I sensed she was ready to go. The doctors had to drain fluid so maybe that's what she's saying about the scar."

"I perceive her as moving forward to stand very close to you now. This typically indicates you were emotionally close in life. She wants you to know she is still close to you, but in a different way, of course."

Anne's eyes fill with tears. "Yes, she and I were very close. She was not only my mom but also my friend. You see, she helped me sort out some painful problems I had not long ago. She was very supportive of me. I miss her so much."

"She says you've felt her around since she crossed over."

"Yes, I have! I didn't know if that was my imagination or not. That's happened when I've been sitting in my favorite chair in the evening."

The woman then begins to impress me with thoughts and feelings about her daughter's life. "Your mom wants you to know she is happy you are no longer in a relationship that really was not good for you. She says that situation was extremely draining for you and you're much better off now. You had to go through this to learn important soul lessons. You've changed so much since then, she says. I trust this makes sense."

"Yes, yes, it does," Anne exclaims excitedly. "I was hoping she would mention this today. It is one of the questions I have written. Does she say anything more about that?"

Through telepathy, I ask the woman to relate more about Anne's relationship. I close my eyes and tune into the communication to be as accurate as possible in giving these impressions.

"Your mom gives me feelings about a betrayal of some sort.

You were shocked and deeply hurt by this when it happened." The woman then shows me the image of an ostrich with its head buried in sand. "She says you tried for a long while to deny what you knew but it was too overwhelming to do so. You could no longer hide the hurt this caused."

Anne nods her head in understanding. "That is exactly what happened. I just couldn't face it. I wanted to believe it wasn't true."

"Was this a marriage or a love relationship?" I ask.

"A marriage," Anne replies, her voice strained with emotion.

The next message that comes through is a difficult one for me to deliver but I feel it rings true. I feel uneasy giving the message but relate it as accurately as I can.

"Your mom gives me strong feelings about your husband. She says he lied all the time and was very manipulative. He was leading a double, secret life, one that you knew nothing about. There were other women involved, she says. He cheated on you many times. Is that right?"

"Yes, he did," Anne responds through tears. "He hid so many things from me over the time we were together. I found out some time later that he was going to prostitutes and viewing porn on the Internet all the time. There were also sexual harassment complaints from women where he works. I still don't know the full extent of everything."

I notice that Anne is visibly trembling. I feel her pain but intuitively know this distressing event is an important part of her spiritual growth. I ask her mom to give more perspective about this.

"Your mom says letting go of him was the best thing you could have done. She gives me impressions about a group you've attended that has helped you do this."

"Yes, that was a group for those involved with people with sexual addictions. Through attending it, I discovered how dependent I was on him. I had to face my denial. I had pretended for a long time that everything was all right but my intuition was telling me a different story. After being in that group, I knew I had to walk away from the marriage. I also meditate and pray every day."

Anne pauses to take a breath.

"I also knew I had to forgive him because of our two kids," she continues. "The anger and hurt were destroying me. The truth is, I'm still working on forgiving him; but the hardest thing I'm facing is forgiving myself for being in such a destructive relationship. I can't believe I didn't see all of this when it was happening. On a deeper level, I know I went through this for a reason. I have to trust that."

"That's not unusual," I comment. "Many people find it easier to forgive others. But it will do you no good to continue to berate yourself, and it will hurt your children, too. Take it one day at a time. There is no reason to criticize yourself any longer. You've learned from it and that's what is important."

"Can you see why this happened?" she asks me. "Do my Akashic records show I had this problem in prior lifetimes?"

I ask Anne's spirit guides for the root of this pattern in her consciousness. In a moment, a vivid impression of Anne wearing a long dress, lace-up boots and a bonnet comes into my inner vision. She appears to have a wound in her stomach that is bleeding. I'm startled by this image and ask Spirit for clarification.

"I'm being shown that you had several past experiences with abusive relationships. In one, you had fear about your physical safety because you were stabbed by your husband then. As a result, you came in this time with a lack of trust in close relationships. Can you see the connection between this and your current life situation? You had mistrust and so attracted someone who was not trustworthy," I explain.

Anne's mouth drops open. "Wow! Yes, it makes sense why I felt I had to take a protection from abuse order against my ex-husband because I feared he would hurt me or the kids. He had been punching walls and throwing things around the house. I was afraid all the time. Am I done with this bad pattern now? I don't want my daughter to go through it."

"Yes, because you have released it through inviting divine awareness into your life through forgiveness," I tell her. "When we forgive, we release the past which stands in the way of our soul's true light. This releases old patterns. Although it may be hard to fathom, you and your husband loved one another enough to plan this lesson together before you were born. He will also grow from this sooner or later. That is up to him."

The session comes to a close. Anne's mother gives one final message.

"Your mom wants you to know she is very proud of you for the growth you've had through all of this. Even though it has been difficult, this situation is a wakeup call for you. Your mom adds that she knows you are a yoga teacher. She loves you very much."

"I got my certification a few months ago to teach yoga! I'm happy she sees that!"

Afterwards, Anne tells me she that she has a clearer perspective of her ex-husband, one that includes compassion, although some of the memories are still painful. She mentions that she is not bitter and maintains a cordial relationship with him, especially where their children are concerned. Because of these past experiences, she has become much truer to her own beliefs and, importantly, has learned to trust her intuition and other people like never before. Her certification to teach yoga strengthened her self-worth and provided the opportunity to bring healing to others.

As conduit for this session, it was inspiring to see the remarkable results brought about by Anne's willingness to forgive a painful betrayal from someone she loved. Fortunately, Anne realized that holding onto these wounds would continue to hurt her and her children.

When we soften our hearts to let go of the past, we are freed to express the divine love that is perpetually anchored within our souls. This is the sparkling vision that Spirit promises us. We owe it to ourselves to take the leap of faith that plants us in the fertile ground of our soul.

Part Three

Your Life Path and Purpose

Nine. Challenges, Growth and Spiritual Evolution

Love is what we were born with. Fear is what we learned here. The spiritual journey is the relinquishment, or unlearning, of fear and the acceptance of love back into our hearts.
~ Marianne Williamson

"What is my purpose in life?" Lori asks me at the start of a reading. "Is there something special I have come here to do? If there is, I don't know what that is. I feel lost and don't know which way to turn. Can you help me?"

Are these questions familiar to you? If you have wondered about your life's purpose, you are certainly not alone. In fact, questions regarding purpose are some of the ones most frequently asked during client sessions. Many people long to discover a deeper meaning to life than superficial concerns. In addition, they want to know how to personally connect with the soul's wisdom by following their inner guidance. Often, this quest arises from a lack of fulfillment with what they mistakenly believe will bring them happiness, like a career, relationship, money or material possessions.

For thousands of years, humans have sought to understand who they are in the grand scheme of life. Seeking purpose in life has steadily increased since the early days in which humankind had to expend enormous effort to simply survive. There was little time to devote to spiritual understanding and pursuits. We face a similar challenge in today's fast-paced, tech-driven world, due to information overload that frequently diverts our attention away from stillness and quiet reflection, both necessary to finding peace and fulfillment within. To discover meaningful purpose, we must detach from the demands of the outside world. For some people, this retreat comes about during times of stress, illness, grief or loss. For others, it results from disillusionment about the superficiality of continually looking outside of oneself to find happiness in money, relationships, notoriety, glamour or substances. Some people choose to withdraw from the busyness of life by taking a vacation or spiritual retreat away from home to quietly contemplate life. It doesn't matter *how* one comes to ask about life purpose; what matters is that one *does* ask this crucial question. For many, asking about purpose is the beginning of awakening to a way of being that transcends societal dictates about satisfaction, prestige, identity and happiness. No one can reveal purpose to us; we must discover it by following our own hearts and intuition. It is the only journey we must take alone in life and one that leads to rich fulfillment if we stay the course.

For many decades, I was confused about my purpose. This intensified when I lost a business to fire over two decades ago. I had invested time, money and sustained effort into a small, local laundromat and dry-cleaning operation that I intended to make successful. After investigating the damage and calculating the cost of rebuilding, I concluded that the business would no longer be viable. My dream of success had literally disintegrated overnight. *Now what was I to do?* I floundered for nearly a year. I wrestled endlessly with the direction to take now that the business was gone.

In my desperation, I went so far as to pray to Spirit to appoint me a job to alleviate my confusion! I didn't care what the job was; I simply wanted to feel much less confused about my direction and enjoy usefulness through working. I wanted the answer and I wanted it now. During this time of soul seeking, I endlessly compared myself to others who appeared to be happy, confident and content. It was only me who felt out of sync with life; everyone else appeared perfectly fine. This judgmental mindset heaped more suffering upon the uselessness I felt. It never occurred to me that my true purpose had little to do with a job or earning money. I had yet to awaken to what that was.

Some months later, I decided to take on several temporary, part-time jobs to pay the bills. One day, I received a phone call from a friend who invited me to attend a nearby metaphysical church. At first I balked and refused the invitation because I thought I'd be wasting precious time. Certainly this wasn't going to help me out of my dilemma. How could attending a spiritual service offer me any insight into what I was to do with my life? After all, I had prayed many times to receive that answer.

I accepted my friend's invitation a few weeks later. Within months, I took several workshops in healing at the church and made plans to attend Delphi University to earn a certificate in mediumship. The rest, as they say, is history. My decision to attend the church opened doors that were previously unimaginable to me. Spirit placed me squarely on a pathway of purpose the moment I released resistance to and preconceived judgments about the process. If I had remained closed-minded, I would not be doing what I do today. Helping others through mediumship has given me immeasurable satisfaction, joy and fulfillment.

My point in sharing my personal story is to assure you that challenging, confusing times where finding direction seems nearly impossible often lead to mental, emotional and spiritual breakthroughs if we open ourselves to receive. Rare is the person who evolves without first experiencing disenchantment and confusion. Human beings are undoubtedly stubborn. We believe we *should* know why we are here, what we are to do and how to go about it. Often, we're expected to know this when we graduate from high school or college. We presume that life should provide us with easy instructions about how to magically obtain the treasures of happiness, peace and fulfilling purpose. When that doesn't happen, we go about seeking these intangible qualities through others, money, places and things where we will never find them. When this ultimately fails, we may become depressed, anxious and hopeless—conditions that rob us of the very things we set out to find.

In today's' world, we are inundated with countless methods and techniques that guarantee quick solutions. Workshops, seminars and books often promise results that, in reality, can only be obtained through the experience of going within for guidance. By no means am I condemning these for they can certainly be signposts that guide us in the right direction. I have developed and taught various workshops myself to help others on their spiritual journeys. Yet in my humble opinion, each of us must courageously take the plunge into our own sacred being to discover lasting, authentic purpose.

Stated another way, we can receive helpful guidance about finding purpose from outside sources like workshops, books, videos and other people but ultimately it is our task to do so. Our soul agreed to take form in the physical world in order to expand and radiate Spirit within. This unique journey is one that requires a deep connection, and familiarity with our own soul, although we can certainly learn from others. Self-exploration without judgment and direct experience lead to the radical shift in consciousness necessary to find and cultivate the array of riches found within.

Change and Spiritual Evolution

In earlier chapters, I reference natural laws—the immutable, timeless principles that govern the universe and the consequences of human behavior. One of these, the natural law of vibration, states that all energy vibrates and changes. That is, nothing is static; energy is constantly moving and evolving. If you were to closely examine the atoms that make up a common object—a table, for example—you would see that this seemingly solid item is comprised of particles that are constantly in motion. This perpetual movement and recycling of energy ensures the survival of the universe as a living entity that continually transforms, expands and evolves. Since we are comprised of this same energy, we, too, are continually evolving, whether we are aware of that or not.

In many cases, the process of internal change is often accompanied by the threat of loss or by loss itself such as the death of loved ones, the end of a job, a life-threatening illness or addiction, serious financial challenges or a debilitating accident. Such crises set the stage for former thoughts and beliefs to transform. These circumstances are wakeup calls (and windows of opportunity) that invite us to explore the very essence of our being.

Crisis precipitated by loss serves us spiritually by opening us to the possibilities of a new way of living. It can reveal to us where we've gone off track by engaging in entrenched thought patterns, not nurturing ourselves, allowing fear to control us, living in the past and future, or forming unhealthy attachments. This is not to say that experiencing any of these necessarily leads to crisis. Grief, confusion, feeling unsettled and being emotionally shaken are natural, human reactions to losing someone or something we cherish. But when these emotional states become extreme because we do not view them from the proper context (as passing states/thoughts and not our core identity), our mind can easily create excessive anxiety, stress and depression.

Unfortunately, these mental states are increasingly common in today's world because we place too much value on interaction with the outer world through technology and other means. On a positive note, modern technology provides us with the ability to connect with people instantly, correspond with others worldwide and take advantage of a vast array of knowledge, information and viewpoints about numerous topics. Curiously, today we are more able to connect with others than ever before, but loneliness and emotional isolation continue to be pervasive, even among those under age 30 who use this technology the most. In the past year, I've seen numerous blogs and articles about "detoxing" from our mobile devices and social media. Who would have dreamed that modern conveniences could modify our thoughts and behavior to the degree that we find it exceedingly difficult to function without them? For some, it's yet another form of addiction. I've read accounts by people who enter a crisis mode when unplugging from their mobile devices and the Internet. It's then they realize just how dependent they've become on technology. Once through the initial withdrawal stage, they regain balance in life by focusing on connections in "real" time instead of virtual ones.

Experiencing crisis can feasibly be the best thing that happens to us in the process of waking up. Let's examine what occurs internally to spur these types of events. Succinctly stated, problems arise when we lose touch with the anchor of Spirit within ourselves and give power to anything else. Problems may not arise for a long while but sooner or later, we feel unfulfilled, sad, angry or depressed. The good news is that when conditions in life inevitably disappoint us, a shift in consciousness occurs, one that lends itself to accessing a different awareness within our own being: the higher consciousness of our soul. This is the valuable role that crisis plays in helping us transform.

It is a mistake to view challenges as obstacles that need to be removed *without first examining what they communicate to and about us.* It is natural to immediately react to these situations with anger, frustration and dismay but if we can instead stand back and view them as portals to the higher self, we can grow in ways that would not be attainable otherwise. This requires acceptance of life exactly as it is. (Read more about how to do this later in this chapter.) It also requires a healthy dose of trust that there are no accidents. Everything we experience has a purpose to move us forward spiritually.

As far as wakeup calls are concerned—specifically, the loss of loved ones—some of the most challenging I have witnessed during readings are deaths of children. Second to this is the loss of a spouse. In both cases, people may be immersed and suspended in grief for months or years. In many cases, the loss of these loved ones creates an indelible shift in the survivors' consciousness that ultimately leads to new awareness of spiritual purpose beyond the pain of loss. This new perception allows for a heightened connection with Spirit through service to help others and the chance to honor the lost loved one's life through various means—all productive ways to use one's life and discover purpose at the same time. Below is an example in which the loss of a child initiated positive changes in grieving family members that led to newfound purpose and healing.

Finding Purpose After Loss

Vincent and Dee come for a session to hear from their son, Josh, who passed six months prior in a car accident. Adding to the immense grief of losing their only son is the manner in which he passed, which was revealed in the reading. Josh had gone out to run a quick errand and his car was hit broadside by a truck. He was killed instantly.

Several times during the session, the parents speak to feeling blindsided by his sudden death and the inability to move beyond their paralyzing grief. I share only the highlights of this session to illustrate the concept of finding new purpose as the result of a tragic event. After Josh comes through and gives multiple validations of his identity and life, he delivers these messages:

"Mom, you ran into a woman, an acquaintance, at the grocery store last week," I relate to Dee. "This woman had heard about my death and said she also lost a son in an accident. She wanted to talk with you more about your feelings. Why did you turn down her invitation to get together? You can help one another by sharing your feelings. Please consider meeting with her."

Judging by the look on her face, Dee is stunned by this message. She responds that no one knew that she had encountered a woman from church she hadn't seen in months while out shopping. She hadn't even mentioned the encounter to her husband. Dee comments that she vaguely recalls the death of this woman's son, although she did not know the family personally.

"Josh must have been there in spirit with me!" Dee exclaims. After she regains her composure from this startling message, she replies, "Um, yes, this is definitely true. I did run into a woman. But I felt uncomfortable talking to her about how I feel. You know, it's not the easiest thing to discuss, right? I guess he's saying this might help me?"

"It appears that way," I respond. "Do you think keeping your feelings and grief bottled up is healthy? It isn't."

"No, I know it isn't. I just don't want to burden anyone."

Josh impresses me with another message. "He says the woman from your church belongs to a group of parents who have lost children. Why don't you ask her to take you to that? It will help you. One of the kids' names is Jake. He's over here with me. You'll meet his parents when you go to the group."

"Oh, I will?" Dee says.

"Yes. He adds that the group also works together on memorials to honor their children's lives. These are projects to help others in your community. Some are speaking engagements, some are acts of service and others are memorial gardens."

"I'd like to build something to keep my son's memory alive," Vincent adds. "He always liked to work with me in carpentry so this would be good to remember him with. I'd really like to build something worthwhile that everyone can enjoy."

"Josh also wants you to know you can sense his presence more clearly by doing meditation. This will bring you peace. Try it and see."

"Do you know why your son is telling you to do all these things?" I ask.

"Well, I guess it's because he loves us," Dee answers. "He was a good son, always helping his dad and me."

"Yes, that's right. But it's also because he knows how much you hurt over losing him. He knows you've both said life is unfair and that you are angry, confused and lost. He doesn't want you to be unhappy. Something good—many things, as a matter of fact—can come from his death. These are your purposes now. These have meaning and will lead to the way out of the dark trench you've been in. Does that make sense?"

Vincent nods. "Yes, it does. For the first time in months, I feel hope. I always said Josh was a smart, caring young man."

"Yes, he certainly is," I say. "He's a spiritually advanced, wise soul."

Afterwards, Dee and Vincent share with me how devastating it was to lose their only son. For many months, they remained paralyzed by grief. Before leaving that day, Vincent tells me that hearing from Josh gave him renewed hope, especially the message about preserving his memory by constructing a wood carving for the front yard of their home. This project makes him feel useful and ready to move forward.

A year or so later, I connected with Dee through e-mail. She told me that she had joined the parents' group Josh had mentioned and had begun several projects, including speaking to other bereaved parents. The teamwork was especially comforting to her since all were working towards the common goal of healing from loss. She looked forward to gaining more peace and purpose from contributing to the group. She left me with these words: "When we lost Josh, I saw no sense in being alive. It was devastating. He is our only child and I will always love him dearly. His messages through the reading gave us what we lacked since he died: peace, hope and purpose."

The Only Constant is Change

If you are like me, you may become anxious when conditions you've grown comfortable with change—despite your best efforts to keep them the same. You may become confused, afraid, angry or disappointed when these changes occur, especially if they are unexpected and beyond your control. It's natural to feel these emotions when we are suddenly confronted with unemployment, the end of a relationship, an unanticipated move, an unexpected depletion of money or the passing of loved ones. How can we confront change with less angst and more resolve to learn and grow from it? Consider the following strategies:

Accept the situation exactly as it is. Resistance is the opposite of acceptance and occurs anytime we want life to be different from what it currently is. Please note that acceptance does not mean that we sit back and do nothing, nor does it mean we have to pretend to like what has happened. What it does mean is that we accept life as it is then make choices about how to proceed. In the useful philosophy of 12-step programs, the first step in coping with challenging change is admitting our powerlessness over anyone or anything other than ourselves. This means we surrender to the current state of "what is." This key step is crucial because it reminds us to assume personal responsibility for our own reaction to life's circumstances. Our reactions to events are the only things we can control.

Acknowledge your feelings. I never advocate ignoring feelings that arise in response to change—or anything else, for that matter. Anger, confusion, sadness, helplessness and grief are all natural feelings most people have during turbulent times. Therefore, in addition to accepting the situation as it is, acknowledge your feelings about it. Denying these will only lead to more problems and block your progress in the long run. Acknowledging your feelings is healthy; wallowing in them creates stopgaps in your progress of coping with change.

Own your responsibility in the change. If we have some

responsibility in contributing to the challenging situation, we must also admit that. For example, if our marriage breaks up, what was our part in making that happen? If we have major financial problems, what did we neglect to see or do about these? Gut honesty is essential. In the case of losing a job, were we ignoring our inner calling to do more fulfilling work? Many times, the universe will move us if don't move ourselves or refuse to heed the calling of our soul. Accepting responsibility (if we have any) gives us power to learn from what we did in creating the challenge. If this step is skipped, we won't understand how the challenge teaches us something valuable about ourselves.

Of course, there are challenges and changes that we have no hand in creating. The death of a loved one is beyond our control. It's likely to take months or years to fully integrate changes that occur during and after grieving the loss of family members, friends or beloved pets. After acceptance of your loss, the next step is the realization of the changes the death has brought to your life. Death is a transition of a soul back to the spirit world and also a transition for the deceased's loved ones who remain in the physical world. Changes will undoubtedly occur as a result of the deceased person's absence from a marriage, family or friendship.

In cases where extensive caretaking of loved ones occurred before death, survivors may be confused, lonely or feel empty in not knowing what to do with their lives when this responsibility ends. This is especially true when people are too consumed by caretaking to connect with others through friendships or spiritual and social support groups. In any of these cases, it's best to make or renew friendships, join groups you're interested in or volunteer with organizations that need help. Reaching out to help others alleviates loneliness and gives purpose to living.

Vow to live one day at a time. This is one of the most practical, useful, stress-reducing tenets I learned in 12-step recovery programs. Living this way makes life much more manageable and far less overwhelming than fretting about the past or worrying about the future. A similar approach is found in the philosophy of Reiki, the hands-on healing modality developed by Usui Shiki Ryoho in the 1930s. This simple, effective technique suggests these basic principles for peaceful living:

- Just for today, I will give thanks.
- Just for today, I will not worry.
- Just for today, I will not be angry.
- Just for today, I will do my work honestly.
- Just for today, I will be kind to my neighbor and all living beings.

(International Association of Reiki Professionals, IARP.org)

Trust that all will work out for the best. Trust is indispensable during times of transition. This is often the hardest attitude for people to grasp in the midst of uncertainty. Trust is the unwavering belief in your soul's innate goodness, which is always present. It is the relinquishment of doubt, fear and personal insecurity to believe in the higher wisdom of Spirit. Trusting that all works out for the best—despite what is happening at the time—replaces helplessness and fear with hope, faith, fortitude and peace.

Trust resides in the still voice within called intuition. When I have taught intuition development workshops, many students have wrestled with trusting their gut over their rational mind. Once they receive confirming feedback from others during practice exercises in the group, trust begins to build. The only way to learn to trust is by making a commitment to do it. When we commit to anything, the universe moves in ways to accommodate and honor that commitment. Our job is to lay the groundwork through our intent and get out of the way.

Mindfulness, Finding Peace and Spiritual Growth

"If only I could get out of debt, secure my dream job, improve my marriage, lose 20 pounds, get along better with my family ..." How often have you thought that if some circumstance in your life changed you could finally attain happiness, success and peace? In many sessions I've given, people want to know how to feel better about life but they have the mindset that something or someone other than themselves needs to change for this to happen. They attempt to solve the "problem" of unhappiness by trying to exert control over that which they have no control.

Since we have no control over anything or anyone other than ourselves, holding onto this sort of wishful thinking is fruitless. In fact, the harder we strive to attain happiness or peace, the more these elude us. This familiar problem brings to mind another basic lesson of truth from the higher awareness of Spirit: genuine peace and happiness comes from within, *beginning with the present moment.* This involves shifting our thinking away from an artificial goal based in the future into appreciation of what is here and now.

How can this be accomplished? Many people have discovered that meditation is an effective tool to help navigate change and overcome stress. All meditation involves calming the rational mind and its constant chatter to reach an expanded state of awareness that transcends the mind. However, many people struggle with meditation because they mistakenly believe its purpose is to stop thoughts entirely or to dispose of thoughts that are already present. In workshops I've taught, people are dismayed and discouraged when they can't get their minds to shut off, or they erroneously believe they need to see "something" through clairvoyance while meditating. They believe they have failed when this is not the purpose of meditation at all.

Did you know there is a particular form of meditation that does not seek to argue with or bypass the mind, but rather acknowledge it? This practice is called **mindfulness.** Some months ago, I found myself consumed by anxiety that came about due to overwork and circumstances in my personal life. There was simply too much on my plate to handle and digest. My mind was on overload with racing, frantic thoughts of the past and future. One particularly stressful night when I was unable to sleep, I silently cried out, *Spirit, please give me peace! I can't handle everything going on. Please, Spirit, give me comfort!*

In the next instant, I heard a voice from within clearly say, *"I'm in your breath. You'll find me there."* I immediately felt comforted knowing my prayer had been heard. Lying in the quiet darkness, I shifted my attention away from my racing thoughts to my breath. I felt relief. I did this over and over each time the anxious thoughts returned. Although I was unaware of it at the time, this crisis "intervention" was my personal introduction to the soothing practice of mindfulness, which I now engage in daily.

While meditation involves shifting our consciousness to transcend the rational mind, mindfulness is the practice of being at peace in the present moment by focusing on the cyclical rhythm of breathing or the current experience one is having. Shifting awareness in this way helps people cope with anxiety, depression, anger, sadness and other frustrating mental states. In addition to practicing mindfulness in short sessions, one can also live daily in mindfulness, bringing focus to the present moment of whatever is happening. Everyday tasks and experiences—vacuuming, washing dishes, bathing and eating— are opportunities to practice mindfulness by bringing present-time awareness to these routine activities. This is accomplished by focusing one's attention on the present-time experience (instead of the breath) one is having.

In the last decade or so, numerous books and audio programs have been written and produced on the value of this simple method of focusing in the present moment with an open attitude of nonjudgmental awareness as to what one is thinking, feeling or experiencing. Two excellent works on this topic are

Mindfulness for Beginners by Jon Kabat-Zinn, PhD (Sounds True, 2016) and *Mindfulness: An Eight-Week Plan for Finding Peace in a Frantic World* by Mark Williams and Danny Penman (Rodale Books, 2012).

Mindfulness practice emphasizes acceptance of whatever one's current experience may be without judgment of that experience. This helps to dissipate distressing thoughts (which produce equally distressing emotions) created by the rational mind, which always strives to solve the problem of what it perceives as "wrong." As most of us have experienced, this overworking of the mind to solve a problem compounds the distressing thoughts, which subsequently begin to build on one another. Soon, we are caught in a spiral of fear, anxiety, grief, anger, hopelessness or sadness. These continue to build and before long, we feel completely done in by these heavy emotions. We feel trapped within our own mind and the thoughts it continually generates. This common problem is the root of mental, emotional and physical ills.

There is no goal in mindfulness; it is an exercise in *being*. The rational mind's primary function is *to do*, to fix, to solve problems, and to find "the answer" to what it perceives is wrong. This function proves invaluable when we navigate through life—learning facts, driving a car, committing items to memory, studying, balancing our checkbooks or inventing efficient ways to accomplish tasks. As noted earlier, the mind has been wired this way through thousands of years of evolution to ensure survival of our species. Yet when it comes to solving the "problem" of painful feelings such as anxiety, grief, loneliness, sadness or anger, the mind is at a loss to find the "answers." Feelings are not problems that need to be solved but rather conditions of being and consciousness that simply exist. Problems arise when we want unpleasant thoughts and emotions to be something other than they are. In doing so, we are fighting against the basic nature of the mind: to solve problems. This resistance produces stress and anxiety. To find answers to unpleasant thoughts and emotions, the mind searches through thousands of memories to compare to our current thoughts and emotions. In that process, we become weighed down by distressing events of the past or we invent an imaginary future where the worst possible outcome occurs.

Mindfulness does not aim to stop the problem-solving function of the mind in any way. Rather it accepts that this is the nature of the mind and at the same time acknowledges that it is also capable of another function: *awareness that it is creating thoughts*. Stated another way, mindfulness brings forth the observer aspect of the rational mind. This allows for space to be created between thoughts and the core essence of oneself as the thinker of those thoughts. Instead of automatically believing every thought we have, mindfulness gives us the perspective to acknowledge a thought's presence as opposed to attaching to it. As observer, we become capable of recognizing we *have* thoughts, but we are *not* those thoughts. This separation is vital to stop the momentum of distressing thoughts from escalating and spiraling out of control.

To illustrate the concept of detachment, consider this analogy: Imagine you are lying on a beautiful, serene beach, gazing at the ocean in the distance. Focus on the waves as they roll towards the beach then recede. From your vantage point on the beach, the waves never touch you; you simply observe them as they continually move in and out. They rise and fall endlessly, blending back into the whole body of water. If you decide to walk towards the shoreline and into the waves, you are affected by them—meaning, you get wet. If you throw caution to the wind and plunge into the waves, you may be drawn under the current and struggle to regain your balance.

Applying this imagery to your mind, the waves represent the endless stream of thoughts that arise in your mind. As the observer on the beach, you are aware of the thoughts as they come up. In other words, you are aware you are thinking. You are the observer of the thoughts but are not directly affected or overtaken by them unless you make the choice to attach to or take them as absolute truth. Herein lies your power point: making the choice to notice your thoughts as they come up, acknowledging them, but not attaching to or necessarily believing them. Each time you make the choice to observe instead of automatically reacting to thoughts, you strengthen your connection to your soul's awareness, which experiences life without judgment. This liberation from your mind's endless thoughts, comparisons and judgments is true freedom of being.

Practicing mindfulness gives us an alternative approach to suffering and to life itself. Fear, anxiety and depression are less likely to take root when regularly engaging in mindfulness because the mind is focused in the present and not in thoughts of the past or future. Present-time awareness places us firmly in the seat of our soul's consciousness, which transcends the rational mind. This same consciousness is what we experience in the spirit world, our real home, where time does not exist. There it is always the present moment. The soul experiences itself in its entirety (including all lifetimes) and through its wholeness as Spirit. We can savor this soothing presence of being through practicing mindfulness daily and staying present in each moment—or at the very least, as much as possible.

Mindfulness Meditation: An Introduction

Below is a short meditation I have personally used to feel better when I've been anxious or distressed. Use this brief exercise daily to center yourself when you feel out of balance or in need of inner peace. Remember, there is no goal to reach, no race to win and no need to be upset when your mind wanders during the process (and it assuredly will). Simply pull your attention back into the present moment by returning your focus to your breath. This exercise should take about seven minutes or so, although you are free to expand it as long as you wish. Read through the meditation a few times before engaging in it.

Begin by resting comfortably. Sit in a chair that supports your spine or lie down on the floor, a mat or a bed. Close your eyes. Hold your entire body in your awareness for a moment. Now focus your attention on your breath as it moves in and out of your body. A good location in the body to gauge this is in your abdomen. Feel the rise and fall of the abdomen as breath comes in and goes out for a minute or so, without forcing it. Now continue to breathe naturally.

Next, focus your attention on your chest. Tune into the breath with each rise and fall of the chest. Notice any sensations that are present in this area of your body. Do not judge anything you feel; simply notice it.

Breathe deeply and shift your attention to your shoulders, neck and head. Explore the sensations present in each, starting with the shoulders and working your way to the top of your head. Feel sensations on your skin, any pressures, aches or tension as well as internal sensations. Take your time to really feel each sensation. Slowly move your attention from the shoulders to the neck, exploring what you feel with each breath.

Expanding your attention to your head, focus on each part of your face: your jaw, lips, cheeks, eyes, forehead and scalp. What sensations do you notice? Perhaps there are none, which is perfectly fine. If your mind wanders off, don't be upset; gently pull it back into the moment by returning your focus to your breath.

Now move your attention to your feet and toes. Following the same process, notice what sensations you observe in this part of your body. Take a deep breath and slowly move your attention to your ankles, calves and thighs, each time noting what is present.

Move your focus now up to your abdomen, again following the movement of your breath with the rise and fall of the abdominal wall. Stay here for a few moments. Don't force anything; just allow this experience to be as it is.

Imagine yourself being held in a loving, warm, encompassing embrace by a physical or spiritual companion who loves you unconditionally. This soul is someone you trust, someone who is always in your heart. Through this connection, you are never alone. Feel yourself held in the perfect peace of knowing that you are a whole, wonderful being, complete in every way.

Slowly return to waking awareness by shifting your attention to the rise and fall of your breath. Be fully aware of this moment. Take a deep breath and open your eyes.

Practicing mindfulness as much as possible will change the very fabric of your life. You will discover that instead of feeling as if life is passing you by, you are living life in greater depth and fullness. After a while, you'll see how you've missed many subtleties in life because your mind was preoccupied with past events or busy chasing a future goal. Eventually, you will discover that you've grown spiritually by letting go of expectations, self-absorption and frustrations about what life *should* be and enjoy what life is *now*.

The Compelling Need for Self-Compassion

Although the topic of compassion has been previously discussed in Chapter 6, I include this section on extending compassion to oneself because many people often neglect this vital step of self-care, although we can greatly benefit from doing so through the elimination of negative self-talk. We give too much weight to the voice of a harsh, inner critic that repeatedly gives us discouraging, deflating messages, like we're not qualified for a job, aren't a loving parent or that our physical appearance is less than perfect. Or perhaps the critic tells us we should feel guilty, put our own needs last or do more because we're not meeting others' expectations. The critic's core message is "I'm not good enough." This self-deprecating inner voice fuels a negative self-image, lack of self-confidence and unrealistic perfectionism.

Eventually, it can lead to an overload of stress, burnout and emotional imbalance. This is why it's vital to nourish oneself with compassion.

As mentioned earlier, I discovered that my ability to express compassion for others has grown remarkably through my mediumship work. This transformation certainly didn't happen overnight, nor did the increased capacity for empathy instantly dissolve annoyances and criticisms I carried towards others and myself. I still had the same personality with all its insecurities, idiosyncrasies, wants and quirks. What eventually changed was my ability to *accept* these parts of myself, no matter how much my mind admonished me for not being perfect. This awakening from believing in an *idea* of spirituality was as profound and necessary as the actual awakening to extend compassion to others. At that point, however, I still had no inkling of the need to give myself compassion. That was to come down the road through the intense wakeup call described earlier.

Early on, I subscribed to the untrue notion that "being spiritual" meant that I could not have negative emotions such as anger, jealousy or sadness, fall into traps set by my ego or fail to get along with others 100 percent of the time. I believed that a truly spiritual person would not engage in any of those behaviors. Where had I gotten such a distorted view of spirituality? In some of the New Age philosophy I had studied years ago, many of these untrue notions were promoted as attributes of a highly conscious person. Within the group of fellow seekers I hung out with in those days, several assumed an air of false superiority as far as being more spiritual than the rest of us. They proudly announced they were done with the "lower" emotions of anger, sadness and jealousy, and much more interested in accessing the higher dimensions of consciousness: joy, unity, peace, spiritual wisdom and unconditional love.

For a time, I bought into these notions about rising above the inferior "earthly" emotions. Worse, I compared myself to the others, berating myself every time one of the lower emotions got the best of me. Looking back now, I know that few of these people had mastery over their own thoughts and emotions; they were merely denying and suppressing them. The truth is that it's impossible to move to higher levels of consciousness if we don't adequately deal with our current level of consciousness. Eventually, I became disillusioned with this façade of spirituality that I had previously thought was genuine. I realized that I needed to focus on the here-and-now as far as my personal lessons were concerned. Thank goodness I woke up before attempting to travel to higher dimensions that others bragged about visiting!

Some time later, I realized that my concept of spirituality was just that: a concept, an idea, not an unfolding experience as it needs to be. I was temporarily done reading and studying about spirituality. Now I needed to *live* it. Further, I made a vow to myself to not engage in relentless self-punishment if I got angry, made mistakes, had an argument with someone or felt sad from time to time.

Down the road, I came to realize that what had been sorely lacking from my direct experience with Spirit was a much-needed steady diet of self-compassion. It seemed far easier to extend that to others, particularly those who came to sessions due to loss. Myself? That was another matter. After all, I still thought I had to be on top of my game all the time. This pattern of caring for others before self is an all too familiar pattern for those of us who work in the healing and intuitive arts. I have talked to many others in the healing arts and the medical field who had to learn to care for themselves first and not last. Ignoring my inner guidance to do so cost me many years of frustration and excessive nervous energy to discover that not looking after oneself is not a noble thing to do; it's counterproductive, exhausting and just plain stupid. On top of that, it's a wonderfully effective way to get ill.

It took the healing crisis of near burnout, emotional depletion and intense anxiety for me to begin to practice compassion towards myself. I was on overload from taking on too much and ignoring my own needs and physical pain. As irrational as it sounds, I was terrified of losing myself beneath the weight of responsibilities if I didn't learn a new way of being—one that embraced and supported my soul. It was once again time to grow. This is when I began a dedicated program of mindfulness through meditation and present-time, focused awareness. We can't count on people and things to change. We must do that work ourselves through self-nourishment. I had to lose myself (the old ways of relating) in order to find myself.

What I learned is that it's infinitely important to be compassionate and gentle with oneself. I like to think of this extension of compassion to self as a wise, steady investment that will pay many dividends. It is not dependent on a fluctuating outside market since it is generated from the unlimited resource of Spirit within. From my observations, we are much too harsh with ourselves. We deny our own needs, believe our own false thoughts or give away our power far too easily. Then we wonder why we are burned out, exhausted, irritable and devoid of purpose.

I encourage you to extend self-compassion by treating yourself as you would a dear loved one: with gentleness, kindness, support and unconditional love. Fill the vessel of your own soul before attempting to serve others. By doing so, you will honor your own needs and offer your best to others.

Ten. Merging Personality and Soul: Offering Your Unique Contribution to the World

Be a lamp, or a lifeboat, or a ladder. Help someone's soul heal. Walk out of your house like a shepherd.

~ Rumi

By now, you may be thinking about how to strengthen and maintain your daily connection with Spirit in a way that is personal, unique and meaningful to you. You may wonder if you have time to introduce the necessary experience of stillness into your busy life to enjoy inner peace, love and harmony. Do you want to learn how to sense and communicate with your loved ones in spirit, your spirit guides and angels? Perhaps you are drawn to do some type of healing work and aren't certain where to begin. No matter where you are now in terms of spiritual awareness, I assure you that you can have the life you want if you make the commitment to realize it, make the time to do so and proceed with small steps to avoid being overwhelmed.

In addition to the teachings discussed in Part Two, other valuable insights about spiritual development have been revealed during sessions and workshops I've presented. They are the focus of this chapter. My intent in sharing these is to help you jumpstart and gauge your own growth, as well as avoid some pitfalls along the way. Hopefully, you will learn, moment by moment, how to transform your current awareness into a deeper alignment with the higher consciousness of Spirit to accelerate your pathway. At some point, you may also discover ways to serve others by using your particular skills, creativity and talents. Please note that there is no pressure to do so, for service (if it is to happen) will naturally evolve as you go along.

One day while scrolling through Facebook, I saw a meme that

made me laugh out loud. To paraphrase, it read: "I meditate. I drink green tea. I burn incense. I practice yoga, and I still want to punch people out." Indeed!

The truth is, awakening spiritually is not a bed of roses. It isn't intended to be or we wouldn't have come into the physical realm in the first place. In the great laboratory called Planet Earth, we cannot expect to gain instant enlightenment, nor are there any shortcuts to growth. There is no race to be run or won. Nothing can be forced; it must evolve naturally, in its own time. Each circumstance that comes our way must be accepted and felt exactly as it is for us to absorb the lesson contained within it. We will certainly endure emotional pain, loss and disillusionment during life, but if we accept these experiences just as they are and give ourselves the latitude to simply sit for a while with our emotions about them, we will discover that troubling events are instrumental in our personal growth and spiritual evolution.

Be True to Self

There is a lesson that's repeatedly come up during my work with mediumship and spirituality: the necessity of being real, genuine and true to oneself. Similar to other vital spiritual qualities, I learned this one through trial and error and by doing just the opposite. For example, when I first began mediumship work, I thought I needed to "try on" different styles of communicating the information received during readings in an attempt to emulate others working in the field. I quickly found this approach was not working out because it felt inauthentic. I soon saw the necessity of discovering my own personal style of delivering messages.

My spirit guides, in their wisdom, knew what I was doing because one day they impressed me with this message through my intuition: "Just be yourself, Carole. You'll see. This will work much better for you."

Admittedly, upon hearing this, I was more than mildly

annoyed at my guides, which is nothing new for me. In fact, in the beginning years of this work, I used to have regular temper tantrums "at them", which I'm sure they found amusing. *Why couldn't they have just told me this from the beginning?* I'd often fume. Although I couldn't see it at the time, they were attempting to spare me discouragement from trying to emulate others in the field. On multiple occasions, I've felt like Dorothy in *The Wizard of Oz* who had to discover that she herself owned the power to return to Kansas. On the other hand, I greatly admire my spirit guides' courage and patience because they obviously took on a tough case when they agreed to work with me!

My own unique style of delivering readings and teaching workshops has slowly evolved from those confusing times in the beginning. To this day, it continues to evolve with each reading. I've often referred to mediumship as a self-upgrading program because that is precisely what happens when diligence and patience are applied to its refinement. I now realize development of my own style couldn't have happened any other way than for me to experience the stark contrast of being true to myself versus imitating others. Although impersonations are effective during stand-up comedy routines, it's no laughing matter when we try to be anyone other than who we are. It may work for a while, but it will eventually leave us feeling deflated, undervalued and empty.

Self-expression and acceptance require that we value and appreciate ourselves exactly as we are. This does not mean we cannot change something about ourselves that we don't like; it means we accept ourselves without harsh criticism, comparisons to others, disapproval or rejection. For most people, it's just as difficult to release self-judgment as it is to give oneself compassion. This stems from fear of not being good enough according to our own or others' standards. We believe that who we are will not measure up in some way and so we hide our self-described deficits for fear of being perceived as weak or vulnerable. But if you consider that condemning yourself serves no purpose other than making you feel worse about yourself, you will understand the fruitlessness of doing so. With an attitude of self-acceptance first, we can make choices about what we want to change. A mindful, hopeful approach to changing the self acknowledges what is currently true for us then looks to existing options for change. Additionally, this approach does not negate or deflate our current way of being, but considers the potential that exists within us.

Self-acceptance embraces our unique personality which, when put into perspective, can be merged with the higher awareness of the soul. This blending naturally occurs during spiritual awakening. You may have heard the expression that the personality should be the servant of the soul and not the other way around. This is true yet sometimes people misconstrue this to mean that the personality should somehow be abolished at a certain point in spiritual growth. Although this may be the case for the ascended masters (The Buddha, Jesus Christ, Lord Krishna) who have settled all karma and no longer have to return to the physical realm, it is not realistic for most of us to think we will relinquish our personality at any stage of life. On the contrary, we can use this aspect of self creatively and effectively in combination with our soul's contribution to the world.

Create a List of Your Soul and Personality Qualities

Many people who ask, "What is my purpose in life?" long to find direction and fulfillment but haven't taken the time or effort to tune into what their personal assets are. It's imperative to take inventory of inner resources — qualities of both personality and soul, including skills and talents — to build awareness of the right direction. Please note: Purpose does not imply a job or career. It *can* mean that but it often does not. Purpose is what feeds and satisfies your soul at its deepest level. Think of purpose as the peace, fulfillment and joy you feel when your soul is fully engaged. Earning money should never be the primary motivation in deciding on your purpose. In fact, placing money above self-fulfillment often diverts us from connecting with real purpose and what makes our soul thrive. You must first find what speaks to your soul at its deepest awareness. The rest will take care of itself. The well-known adage, "Do what you love and the money will follow," is true.

There are two types of qualities we possess: those flowing directly from our soul and those we express through our unique personality. We need to combine these throughout life to maintain mental, emotional and spiritual balance. Do not fall into the trap of believing you will come out ahead by suppressing or negating your personality while doing spiritual work. As mentioned previously, some people mistakenly believe that awakening spiritually means leaving human emotions and the personality behind. This erroneous mindset is capable of producing false superiority to others. I've personally witnessed people working in the healing arts who have unwittingly succumbed to this way of thinking tumble from the self-imposed "holier than thou" pedestal they imagined themselves to be on. When that happens, it's never pleasant to watch. It's key to accept *all* aspects of self—including your unique personality.

During my early training at Delphi University in the late 1990s, one of my teachers, Patricia Hayes, taught us that an efficient way to tune into people prior to giving readings is to focus on their most prominent soul qualities like compassion, patience, humility, integrity, love, nurturing, generosity, wisdom or kindness. Patricia advised us to choose three qualities that stood out when we looked into the eyes of the person to be read. Once these were acknowledged, the reading would then begin to flow because we had connected with the other's seat of higher wisdom, the soul. I've used this same exercise with good results while training students during workshops in intuition and mediumship development. When doing this exercise, it's helpful to use the faculty of clairsentience (feeling) to sense what qualities the soul expresses.

To gain clarity, spiritual direction and personal insight, I suggest you make a list of your own soul qualities. You can tune into your own or others' soul qualities by using your intuition. To do this, have paper and pen handy before closing your eyes, placing your hand over your heart and asking Spirit to speak to you directly through your soul. Focus on your breath and tune into what you sense, hear or feel from this quiet voice of wisdom within. What qualities does your soul express? If you stand back and look at your life, what qualities enabled you to have rewarding relationships, raise a family, navigate difficulties, volunteer or succeed at a business? Listen with your intuition to receive these impressions. Write at least three qualities that you perceive.

Writing brings clarity to feelings, sensations and ideas that are vague. Approach this exercise with your full attention and genuine curiosity, much as if you were meeting and getting to know someone for the first time. There is no judgment here, no right or wrong answers. It is an investigation into self, plain and straightforward, to acknowledge the resources you possess. Often, our overly critical minds don't permit us to see the abundance of good we already enjoy. Now is the time to remove those blinders and see yourself clearly through the eyes of your higher self without reserve or guilt.

After doing the soul quality exercise, explore what unique qualities you express through your personality. The difference between soul qualities and those of the personality is that the latter is the specific, unique flair you bring to life. The personality is what adds your individual flavor, spice and pizzazz to what you are expressing or doing. For example, are you witty, humorous, creative or adventurous? Are you intelligent, well-spoken, sincere, committed or honest? Do you have a knack for putting others at ease? Are you helpful to others? Are you communicative, quiet or thoughtful? Ask a friend to give positive feedback if you're having trouble seeing what these might be. To use another angle, think about how you would honestly describe yourself on a dating website. What characteristics about you stand out? After describing these, write them on a sheet of paper separate from your soul qualities.

Now take both sheets of paper and see what qualities on each harmonize, support and reinforce one another. For instance, if you have the soul quality of wisdom and the personality quality of being communicative, teaching or writing may be a likely calling for you. Another example would be the soul quality of kindness merged with the personality quality of enjoying service to others. Perhaps this points toward practicing the healing arts, such as hands-on healing, giving readings or working with plant medicine. If you have a creative flair personality-wise and also express the soul quality of compassion, you may be drawn to paint, sew or make jewelry to donate to charity. If your soul naturally nurtures others and you like children, you might volunteer or work as a teacher's aide or become involved in organizations that serve children or young people. Don't concern yourself with how any of this will come about. Your task is to simply identify the direction you need to move towards.

Next, consider how you might begin to bring these new insights into reality. This will lay the foundation for the changes you want. What is one small thing you can do today to make that happen? Don't overthink; allow the information to sink into your awareness. Be specific and take action in faith, one day at a time. Don't worry about how or when results will happen; the mind of Spirit is far greater than our own in its ability to manifest results. Trust it. Your intent to know yourself at a deeper level has already opened the door to higher awareness of purpose. Trust that you will be guided to answer the call of your soul.

As you examine the two sets of qualities you express, you will begin to see an alignment between how your soul expresses itself and the specific signature of your unique personality. Now that you have made the effort to bring this awareness into your consciousness, step back from this assessment, surrender to the infinite wisdom of Spirit and continue to build your spiritual power. Trust that all answers will come as you are ready for them. All is in divine order.

Resources to Power Up Your Spiritual Awareness and Connection

In addition to mindfulness meditation, which we've already discussed, there are other practices and experiences that will help you develop intuitive awareness. These increase awareness of spiritual energy in everyday life, cost nothing and are easy for anyone to access. They will help you to recognize and embrace the encompassing presence of Spirit manifesting in the physical world.

Connect With Nature. Plants, trees and flowers radiate the perfection, majesty and stillness of spiritual energy without thought or language. Someone once said that if you want to find yourself, get lost in nature. Being outdoors creates appreciation for the glorious forms that Spirit inhabits in the physical realm. A refreshing experience is to walk outdoors and tune into the sights, sounds and sensations that surround you. See if you can simply notice and enjoy these without engaging your thinking mind, much like a child. Imagine that this is the first time you are exploring this particular path or route; everything is new, intriguing and exciting. What is your experience? What do you sense, feel, hear?

Nature inspires us with the spiritual quality of non-judgment because it simply *is*. It does not require a name, label or endorsement to exist. It is an elegant expression of the higher mind of Spirit. When we spend time in nature, we remember the virtues and beauty of our own soul without the impingement of the mind. Being in nature also allows us to detach from distractions that demand our attention such as mobile devices, work obligations and the chatter of TV.

If you are unable to get outdoors, you can instead "bond" with a plant in your home. Without thinking too much, study the plant with your eyes to notice details about it. Note the shapes, colors and conditions of the leaves, stems or flowers (if there are any). Then close your eyes and touch a part of the plant. Focus on the texture, weight and temperature. If you really want to tune in, ask the plant for a message. What is revealed? Don't feel silly about doing this; modern scientific studies offer ample evidence that plants, trees and flowers can indeed silently communicate using their own language. (This has been demonstrated through electronic devices that measure the frequencies emitted by the plants they are wired to.) Much like receiving messages from those in the spirit world, it's a matter of tuning in to receive what is being broadcast by the plant. When I have done this exercise, I've noticed an active presence that emanates from trees, plants and flowers. I feel the aliveness of Spirit within the form, without thinking or analyzing it. Use your intuitive senses to feel the essence residing within flowers, plants and trees. You will discover an alert intelligence that is present in each.

Each blade of grass, leaf, bark, twig and insect is a manifestation of the vital energy of Spirit, the very same substance that is within you, me and the entire universe. The only difference is the physical form this energy takes. Recognition of this oneness and collaboration in nature is a profound awakening into the sacred interconnectedness of all of life. Nothing and no one is isolated; everyone and everything is connected. We share relationships with everyone and everything, even if we never make physical contact with them. What affects one, affects all. Knowing these truths changes our perspective on life from one of separation, division and aloneness (stemming from the mind) to one of unity, cohesiveness and cooperation (Spirit).

Befriend Non-Human Beings. Animals bring their own wonderful inspiration as the embodiment of Spirit. Over the course of my life, I have received inestimable, uplifting, encouraging lessons from animals of all species. I've also studied about communicating intuitively with animals, which is possible due to the unity of all, irrespective of species. Although animals' language differs from ours, there is definite communication taking place between animals themselves as well as between animals and humans. A good resource for learning to communicate intuitively with animals is *Pets Tell the Truth* by Agnes Julia Thomas (Hanover Publishing, 2005). In addition to giving instruction and methods to learn animal communication, the author also shares teachings about pets and the afterlife, reincarnation of pets and the human-animal bond.

If you have pets, you understand just how skilled they are at knowing your thoughts and sensing your moods. To sharpen your intuition, try tuning into a pet's thoughts to communicate with him through clairvoyance. It's best to have his full attention when attempting this, perhaps with him sitting directly in front of you. Look into his eyes and face. Send a mental image of something familiar to him by thinking of it (for example, a favorite treat or toy). Then tune in to receive his response or reaction. What do you see or sense? What is his response in terms of movement or behavior? Listen through your intuition to pick up mental images he might send to you. Don't be discouraged if you don't receive a message at first. Just as "human" mediumship takes dedication and practice, communicating with animals requires the same discipline.

Animals are powerful sources of inspiration because much like nature, they are a genuine, nonjudgmental expression of Spirit. They bring spiritual presence naturally without using the thinking mind or engaging in pretenses. This is why their connection with humans is restorative and healing, especially for those who suffer from physical and mental illness, trauma or abuse. Interacting with them instills us with purity, comfort and reassurance.

Therapy dogs have long been trained to help humans with physical, emotional and mental challenges. Other animals are also capable of making special connections with humans. Miniature horses, for example, are also being specially trained for therapy services, primarily for children. These beautiful, tiny equines offer encouragement, hope and healing for anyone with life-threatening illnesses, elders in assisted living facilities, and those affected by natural disasters and other crises. The magnitude of their spirit shines through these minis' bright eyes and quiet demeanor. I've personally felt their healing power even through the computer screen. (To learn more about these special horses, visit gentlecarouseltherapyhorses.com.)

Join Groups with Like-Minded Others. Becoming active in various groups is another resource that can help you refine your spiritual awareness. Over the years, I've gone to many groups in which various metaphysical topics and healing modalities were explored. Groups are an excellent resource for learning and exchanging ideas with others of like mind who can become trusted sources of friendship and support. A few well-respected international groups to explore are Unity (unity.org), Centers for Spiritual Living (csl.org/en) and Eckankar (eckankar.org). It's easy to find online groups by typing "spiritual support groups" into your search engine. Before attending, it's wise to research groups to make certain they are what they claim to be. You can use online resources, ask others in your circle about their personal experiences or contact the organizations themselves for further information.

Small gatherings have also been part of my growth, learning and experience. I've attended many Reiki exchanges, been a member of a hands-on-healing team and joined in spiritually based book study groups. To find groups like these in your local area, search online by your city or town or reach out to your network for referrals through word of mouth.

Lift Your Thoughts to a Higher Vibration. Shifting your awareness to higher consciousness begins and ends with the thoughts you have. Most of us are familiar with the adage that our thoughts create our reality. Since this is true, if we want our life to be different (the effect), we must first change our thoughts (the cause). Because thoughts are energy and all energy vibrates at a particular frequency according to its composition (dense, light or somewhere in between), all thoughts have a rate of vibration and charge to them.

The law of attraction states that a frequency of energy pulls similar and identical frequencies to it. Since thoughts are energy, each has the ability to attract similar or identical thoughts. For example, this is how the spiral of anxiety mentioned in the previous chapter is created. Thoughts are interconnected and layered. This appears to be especially true with self-defeating thoughts. Take the example of a repetitive thought, "I'm a failure at love." This thought could potentially spiral and build in intensity as other thoughts similar to it arise within my mind. Typically, these are corresponding thoughts and beliefs based in the past, which seem to support the original thought. In this example, these might include, "Past partners saw who I really was (unworthy) and left me," or "I'm not deserving of anyone's love because I'm unattractive, overweight or stupid," or "I am unlovable because neither of my parents showed me affection, love or attention." In the course of seconds, we can shift through layer after layer of thoughts with the same negative charge. By the time we're done, we feel drained, defeated and hopeless. This spiral of escalating thoughts must be interrupted to break free of the bad feelings associated with such thinking.

On the flip side, uplifting thoughts attract others of the same vibration. The more we think self-affirming thoughts and kind thoughts about others, the more these positive thoughts build and attract similar thoughts. This is also a spiral but one that is much easier to live with compared to the ones created by negative thinking. Since we create our reality based on the quality of our thoughts, thinking uplifting thoughts corresponds with harmonious conditions in life.

Each thought validates and reinforces your unity with Spirit—or, at the opposite end of the spectrum, your mind's perception of separateness from that universal source. Holding thoughts of love, peace, kindness, helpfulness and forgiveness lifts your consciousness closer to divine consciousness. Thoughts of a lower vibration (hatred, anger, vindictiveness, division or jealousy) take you farther away from Spirit. The body reacts in accordance with the thoughts we have, either tightening up and constricting, or opening up and relaxing. Experiment with this by tuning into how your body reacts when you think uplifting thoughts and then switch to negative ones. With the latter, you may notice your heart beating faster and harder, your breath becoming shallow, your muscles tightening and your skin perspiring. This is because negative thoughts create stress since they are in conflict with your true nature: love. In time, they take a toll on the body and can produce illness.

On an energetic level, your **aura** (the energy field surrounding your body) expands when you generate positive, harmonious thoughts and contracts when you think negative, divisive ones. Thoughts carry either a positive or negative charge that affects ourselves, others and the environment around us. We continually broadcast energy into the atmosphere and universe. This is why we often receive whatever matches our thoughts. For instance, if I continually have fears about being alone, I will probably feel unloved, unwanted or bored when forced to spend time alone. Or I could attract people who abandon me in relationships. Another possibility is that I will seek unfulfilling or unhealthy relationships simply to avoid being alone.

During a metaphysical seminar I attended years ago, the instructor demonstrated the power of thoughts and their charge in the aura with **divining rods**, thin copper or twig pieces in either an L or Y shape, loosely held in the hands at one end, with the other end swinging freely. Over the centuries, this device has been used to locate underground water but can also be used to sense and detect the quality and width of energy around a person.

In the case of using the rods to locate water, the free ends of the rods open widely and fall apart when water is near. During the demonstration, a volunteer was instructed to think thoughts of a relatively lower vibration like anger, sadness or hatred. The instructor held the rods a foot or so away from the volunteer's body. As we watched with astonishment, the rods closed tightly together. Next, the same volunteer held thoughts of a high vibration: someone they loved, something they were grateful for and a specific instance in which they felt comforted or at peace. In a few seconds, the rods swung widely apart in the instructor's hands. The demonstration was then repeated with a second volunteer with similar results.

Later that day, I tried the experiment myself with a friend. (I was a little skeptical that the instructor may have subconsciously, innocently manipulated the rods much like one could unconsciously move a planchette—a pointing device used on a Ouija board to spell out words.) So to discover the truth for myself, I held the rods while my friend thought about a heated argument she'd had with a relative. The rods immediately clamped tightly together in my hands. Next, she thought loving and appreciative thoughts about her husband and dog. The rods opened widely in my hands. The difference in the width between the rods was astonishing.

Have you heard the expression, "I could feel her when she walked into the room"? People are aware (often unconsciously) of the scope and consistency of others' auras. Most people are attracted to those who radiate uplifting qualities and repelled by those who hold lower energetic emotions. You own the power to choose what you will give your attention to at any given moment which determines the quality of your thoughts.

Some people do not realize that they are in charge of the quality of their own thoughts. Others know this but do not use the power of choice and instead fall into unconscious habitual reactions that are often self-defeating. Most of us give far too much attention and weight to our own negative mental patterns, our past reactive conditioning, others' opinions, and the promptings of society and the media. Although we do not live in a vacuum (nor should we), the only truth we need be concerned with is the substance of our own thoughts because this is the only thing we truly command. The world will always have its distractions, sorrows and pain, but we get to decide what to focus on in our inner world. Knowing we have this choice and not succumbing to being a victim of a supposedly harsh, uncaring world is one of the signs of spiritual maturation.

How to Raise the Vibration of Your Thoughts

How do we get from where we are to higher ground? Begin by experimenting with raising the vibration of your thoughts by choosing something small that you'd like to change. It's not the size or extent of the changes you make that matters as much as the attitude you bring when making those changes. It's helpful to first reflect on the way you think by logging thoughts you commonly have in a journal. Do you have habitual thoughts that repeatedly cause you distress? Writing about these will help you to clearly identify them and note changes as you move through the process step by step:

- Choose a single thought that creates mildly unpleasant feelings for you. This doesn't have to be something of major importance. Choose a thought that you'd like to modify to feel more comfortable when it arises; for example, "I'll never have enough time to get everything done today."

- As you think your chosen thought, notice what distressing feelings come up. In the example above, you might feel anxious, stressed, impatient or defeated. Take note of how you feel and, importantly, how the thought affects your body. Every thought we have is reflected in our body, even though these changes may be subtle. Does your chest tighten or your breath become shallow? Tune into your facial expressions by saying the thought aloud in front of a mirror. How does this thought affect your demeanor? Write these observations in your journal.

- Ask yourself if the thought rings true and is valid. To do this, question yourself about it. In the sample thought above, you would ask if it is true that you definitely won't accomplish everything you need to do today. How do you know this is true? Is it a fact based on an outside factor, known information or did you already decide you won't accomplish what needs to be done? If so, how do you know that? Or is this thought a projection of your own fear of not being able to meet these demands? Are the things on your to-do list able to be reasonably accomplished by day's end? Or are you taking on too much and adhering to an unrealistic standard? Too often we believe in thoughts that hold no validity except in our own mind.

- See if you can reframe this thought into something more positive. In the example, you could change it to a more affirming one like, "I will use today to accomplish what I can, one step at a time," or "I will accomplish all I have to do today and have time to spare."

- Note your feelings after changing the thought to a less stressful one. Check into the sensations in your body. What do you notice as you speak the new thought aloud in front of a mirror? Note your posture and demeanor. How do these feel?

- Practice replacing the original thought with the new thought each time it arises. Don't be hard on yourself if the old thought returns; simply bring awareness to it and replace it with the new thought. Recognizing defeating thoughts as they arise is half the battle of transforming them into more positive ones.

Here are some additional ways in which you can raise the vibration of your thoughts slowly over time:

- Begin and end each day by thinking about at least five things you are grateful for. Find someone or something beautiful to appreciate. You won't have to search very long to find this as there are many. Remember that focusing on gratitude increases the flow of abundance.
- Think kind thoughts and perform kind acts to help others. Consider these thoughts: *"If I were this person what would make me feel better?"* or *"If I were the one in this situation or circumstance, what would I appreciate help with?"* Then do that thing without expectation of return. No act of kindness is ever lost because everything we give to others will return to us, sooner or later.
- Practice the divine quality of humility. Realize that you are no better or worse than anyone else. We are all Spirit's children. Humility diminishes self-centeredness and promotes open-mindedness and the willingness to learn.
- Engage in forgiveness. Carrying the weights of hurt, resentment, anger and bitterness are not compatible with higher consciousness. Practicing forgiveness is your ticket to spiritual freedom and the key that unlocks healing. Shift thoughts of blame into ones of acceptance by adopting the perspective that everyone you encounter on your pathway is a contributor to your growth and experience. You might

also ask what you learned about yourself if the situation is painful. Take this wisdom and grow from it.

- Practice non-judgment. Be at peace by accepting your life without judgment of self or others. Thoughts of resistance to your current reality create tension, anxiety and anger. This, in turn, creates more resistance. Practice observing your life without labeling it as "worse", "sadder" or "unluckier" than others'. Comparisons dim the light of your soul. Learn to see yourself and others in a balanced light. Most of us have redeeming qualities along with those we still need to work on. No one is perfect. As a divine being, marvel at your own inherent value and uniqueness. You can be no other place than at the right place at the right time.

- Post reminders of the "new" thoughts where you will see them daily. A good place to place them is on your bathroom mirror where you will see them at the start and finish of each day.

Your Greatest Accomplishment

How would you respond if someone asked you about your greatest achievement in life? Would you answer with something career-related, such as earning a coveted promotion, being the head of a department, commanding a high salary or working many years for the same company? Would your response be recognition of some sort: a medal, honor, award or perhaps a college degree? Have you earned awards in sports? Many people consider raising a family to be their greatest achievement, a noble accomplishment for certain. If you were to die tomorrow, what can you say now that you've accomplished that is most meaningful to you?

To be clear, nothing is wrong with any of these admirable accomplishments. As we awaken spiritually, however, we tend to reset our priorities to become less focused on outer accomplishments and more concerned with inner qualities such as peace, forgiveness, compassion and selfless service. Many outer achievements can and will change over time. We eventually retire from working, put our awards away and experience our children growing up and moving out. Yet regardless of what changes take place on the outside, you can ground yourself in the anchor of what you have accomplished *within*, the qualities you embrace and express that are direct reflections of the beauty of your soul. No one can give you these qualities and no one can take them from you. Over time, these inner accomplishments often deepen and give an elevated richness to life that surpasses anything we've earned externally. Indeed, these are the only real, non-tangible accomplishments you will take to the spirit world upon death, as many in spirit have revealed to me.

In thousands of sessions, I've yet to hear spirits prioritize earthly values such as money, work or possessions over love, kindness, service, forgiveness or generosity. I've never heard a spirit say, "I wish I would have worked longer hours or earned more money." In spiritual awareness, these practical concerns are at the bottom of the list. Unfortunately, many people come to sessions with those very concerns: worries about money, property, the distribution of inheritances and family disagreements over these matters. This contrast in priorities speaks to the radical difference between earthly perspectives and those from the soul's vantage point. When all is said and done, you alone are responsible for the quality of your life, which you will witness through your soul review in the spirit world. There you will see the impact that your life had on others, the lasting legacy you leave to the material world through the service you gave from your heart.

In the days ahead, don't become discouraged by the inevitable bumpiness of the road you walk during your continued spiritual awakening. This is not a straight, easy path. Remember, much of your life was planned by your soul for its evolution. When life is the most difficult, see past the illusions of hopelessness, fear and defeat by listening to the voice of Spirit through your soul. Instead of blaming others, look carefully for the soul lessons contained within each circumstance. You won't be as discouraged or disappointed if you take this elevated perspective.

While a spiritually centered life is not necessarily an easy path, it's also true that it is not serious work all of the time. Invite lightness into your life through laughter, playfulness and things that bring you joy. His Holiness The Dalai Lama regularly smiles, laughs heartily and tells jokes when he speaks. When he was asked in a CNN interview why he is so playful, he responded, "It's important for leaders, particularly spiritual leaders, to act like human beings and to be playful."

Realize that you are always accompanied by loved ones who travel beside you in spirit—your family, companions, guides and teachers. Along the way, they will remind you that living on the physical plane is a dream and dying is waking from that dream. Know that these souls are not superior to you but rather teammates helping you to be the loving soul you were born to be. Remember the eternal bond of love unites you with those you have known and loved.

Develop and learn to trust your direct line to higher awareness: your intuition. While it's easier to give way to outside distractions and follow the crowd many times, nothing can replace the inner voice of wisdom that will reliably steer you to your higher self. By following this route, your purpose as a loving soul will clearly shine forth.

Humbly share your personal challenges, insights and experiences with others who can benefit from them. By doing so, you will uplift, encourage and assist others to see Spirit within themselves. You have much to offer others who are new to the journey of developing spiritual awareness. Don't hesitate to show it!

Do not limit or define yourself by holding onto the past. Forgive yourself and others daily and move forward. You are far greater than any of the wounds you have endured. These cannot dim the light of your soul in its brilliancy.

Remember that you came to the physical realm to radiate the power and presence of Spirit. Let the light of your soul be apparent to all through service, compassion and love. You will never regret extending yourself in this way.

When you return home one day, you will see your soul's unique contributions to humanity and the indelible impressions they've left on the world. Until then, live freely, be at peace and give way to your heart.

About the Author

Carole J. Obley has been the bridge between heaven and earth in more than 9,000 group and individual readings. She is the author of three books on spirit communication, spirituality and healing.

Carole has published articles on spiritual and metaphysical subjects and taught numerous workshops at Lily Dale, New York, the largest center for Spiritualism in the United States. She has been the subject of various newspaper articles and spoken on both radio and TV.

Ms. Obley holds a certificate in mediumship from Delphi University in Atlanta, Georgia and has a mastership in Reiki healing. She has produced audio programs to help people with spiritual development and teaches three levels of classes in intuition and mediumship.

Carole is the founder of Soulvisions, LLC, an ethical company dedicated to helping people find peace and healing through evidential mediumship. Soulvisions also offers books and audio programs about mediumship and presents workshops and seminars on developing intuition, metaphysics and spirituality.

To learn more, visit soulvisions.net.

Other Books by Carole J. Obley

Embracing the Ties That Bind: Connecting With Spirit
(Xlibris, 2003; ISBN 1-4010-8971-2)
In this inspiring guide to self-discovery, spiritual medium and healer Carole J. Obley leads you in an enlightening journey of healing and empowerment through helping you connect with your intuitive awareness beyond your five physical senses. She shows how you can use the power of your thoughts to understand and heal karma from your past lives, speak with your angels and guides, tune into the spirit world and attract prosperity. Personal experiences of the author and intriguing revelations received through direct communication with the spirit world make this book a *must* read for spiritual seekers everywhere.

I'm Still With You: True Stories of Healing Grief Through Spirit Communication (6ᵗʰ Books, 2008;
ISBN 978-1-84694-107-8)
A collection of compelling, true stories of after-death communication from the experiences of psychic medium Carole J. Obley. These inspiring examples open our hearts and minds by convincingly demonstrating how contact with the spirit world can be a catalyst in healing grief. We are uplifted and comforted by realizing that the challenges we face in life can be positively transformed by the magnificent strength of undying love.

Soul to Soul Connections: Comforting Messages From the Spirit World (6ᵗʰ Books, 2013; ISBN 978-1-84694-967-8)
Is it possible to heal relationships with deceased loved ones and grow spiritually in the process? How do we release our emotional hooks and hurts that keep us painfully attached to the past? In *Soul to Soul Connections*, spiritual medium Carole J. Obley shows us how we can transform unfinished business from the past into

profound spiritual understanding and experience true freedom of being. By sharing inspiring, real stories from her extensive case files of direct communication with clients' deceased loved ones, Ms. Obley compassionately leads us into our own heart and soul to relinquish guilt, anger, grief and fear. This book offers healing and comfort to anyone wanting to forgive and feel at peace.

Glossary

Agape – The highest form of love; the love Spirit has for humankind and the love humankind has for Spirit.

Akashic Files – The energetic codes of the totality of a soul's consciousness, including each lifetime, in between lives, karma and blueprints; also called the Akashic Records.

Angels – Divine beings who interact with humankind to assist in its spiritual evolution. Angels have never been in human form. Their mission is to carry out the will of Spirit. As extensions of pure, divine consciousness, they are not subject to karma. There are many classifications of angels, each concerned with a different aspect of spiritual consciousness. Our **guardian angel** is with us from birth, ensuring our protection and helping us with our divine life plans.

Ascended Masters – Souls who have completed their earthly lessons but continue to assist humankind with its spiritual evolution from the higher realms of Spirit. They are no longer subject to karma and reincarnation since they have mastered the lessons of the physical dimension. Examples are Jesus, The Buddha and Lord Krishna.

Aura – The electromagnetic energy field emanating from and surrounding a living being. The aura changes in quality, consistency and strength based on the thoughts, feelings and health of the individual.

Blueprints – A soul's plan, outline or design for physical life. Blueprints are formed before each incarnation.

Clairaudience – The spiritual ability to hear non-physical communication through telepathy.

Claircognizance – The spiritual ability to know current or future events without physical evidence.

Clairsentience – The spiritual ability to feel emotions of others both on earth and in spirit; the ability to receive sensations produced by spirit beings in one's body. Examples are sadness, guilt and joy, or bodily sensations such as tightness in the chest, headache or leg pain.

Clairvoyance – The spiritual ability to see images and scenes using the mind's inner eye.

Divining Rods – A Y-shaped single twig or rod or two L-shaped rods first used in 16th Century Germany to detect underground water and buried metal.

Ego – The individualized aspect of universal consciousness. It is the personal mind—who you are as a unique being distinct and/or separate from the unity of Spirit.

Higher Self – Another term for the soul, the perfect essence of Spirit.

Karma – Cause and effect; from Sanskrit, "action." The natural law that dictates that what we create (thoughts, words, and actions) we receive.

Law of Attraction – A universal, impartial principle which states that the magnetic power of the universe draws similar energies together. In metaphysics, the frequency of our thoughts draws similar frequencies to us.

Life Review – The "replay" of a soul's physical life which takes place after entry into the spirit world upon death. This assessment includes the impact a soul's thoughts, words and actions had on others.

Magnetic Resonance – In metaphysics, the attraction of similar or identical thoughts. It is interconnected with the Law of Attraction; we attract frequencies of thought that correspond to ours. It is the attraction between souls who share similar states of consciousness and/or between those who have made pre-birth agreements to evolve together.

Master Teachers – In theosophy, a human being who has become unified with Spirit through passing initiations (spiritual tests) on the earth. Master teachers are ascended souls who no longer are subject to karma and the wheel of reincarnation, but continue to aid humankind in its spiritual evolution. They assist humankind in its quest for unification with Spirit through imparting specific wisdom and teachings to that end.

Mindfulness – The practice of focusing one's consciousness in the present moment away from thoughts about the past and future. Although there are various forms of mindfulness, most use one's breath to bring awareness to present time.

Natural Laws – A body of timeless, immutable principles governing the universe and the consequences of human behavior. There are seven natural laws: mentalism, correspondence, vibration, polarity, rhythm, cause and effect, and gender.

Numerology – A branch of knowledge that deals with the mystical significance, properties and symbolism of numbers. Many numerologists credit the Greek philosopher Pythagoras as the first to study numbers, their mystical meanings and applications of these to the universe.

Querant – A person seeking insight and guidance through divination and consultation with an oracle; for example, the Tarot.

Reincarnation – The theory that souls have multiple lifetimes in the physical world for the purpose of evolving spiritually. The concept is also referred to as "the wheel of life." Hinduism and Buddhism are two major religions that adhere to this belief.

Ripple Effect – The phenomenon of one soul's expression affecting many others. It is similar to the Butterfly Effect, whereby a small change in a large system produces far-reaching effects in that system.

Shadow Self – Aspects of the personality that are repressed because of denial, shame or fear.

Soul Agreements – Lessons planned by two or more souls to interact for the purpose of spiritual growth.

Soul Group – Beings who share a similar spiritual consciousness. We frequently meet with our soul group from lifetime to lifetime as well as in between lives. These souls may be biological family members, friends, co-workers or other souls with whom we have prearranged lessons.

Spirit Guides – Souls who have agreed to help humans (before birth) during physical incarnation. Often, we know these helpers from previous incarnations or they are members of our soul group.

Spiritualism – A system of belief based on the premise that the spirit is eternal and communication with those in the spirit world is possible through the assistance of a medium. Hands-on-healing is also practiced in many Spiritualist churches. Spiritualism is recognized and practiced as a religion throughout the United States, Canada and the United Kingdom, as well as other countries.

Synchronicity – The simultaneous occurrence of two seemingly unrelated events that holds significance for the receiver. There is speculation that synchronicity is the intelligent universe reflecting our thoughts and experiences back to us.

Tarot – A system of 78 cards with four suits of minor arcana (each representing one of the four elements: water, earth, air and fire), 22 major arcana (archetypes in the human psyche and the soul's journey) and 16 court cards (representative of people in the querant's life or qualities of the energy of the suit they are from) that is used for insight, spiritual guidance and divination.

Teaching Spirits – Souls (including our loved ones in spirit) who instruct us with specific guidance concerning spiritual development.

Wakeup Calls – Crises such as physical or mental illness, accidents, divorce, death of a loved one and job loss that can positively serve as portals or breakthroughs in our consciousness for spiritual growth.

Windows of Opportunity – Situations and events that serve as catalysts and portals to develop higher spiritual consciousness.

6TH BOOKS

ALL THINGS PARANORMAL

Investigations, explanations and deliberations on the paranormal, supernatural, explainable or unexplainable. 6th Books seeks to give answers while nourishing the soul: whether making use of the scientific model or anecdotal and fun, but always beautifully written.

Titles cover everything within parapsychology: how to, lifestyles, alternative medicine, beliefs, myths and theories.

If you have enjoyed this book, why not tell other readers by posting a review on your preferred book site? Recent bestsellers from 6th Books are:

The Afterlife Unveiled

What the Dead Are Telling us About Their World!

Stafford Betty

What happens after we die? Spirits speaking through mediums know, and they want us to know. This book unveils their world...

Paperback: 978-1-84694-496-3 ebook: 978-1-84694-926-5

Spirit Release

Sue Allen

A guide to psychic attack, curses, witchcraft, spirit attachment, possession, soul retrieval, haunting, deliverance, exorcism and more, as taught at the College of Psychic Studies.

Paperback: 978-1-84694-033-0 ebook: 978-1-84694-651-6

I'm Still With You

True Stories of Healing Grief Through Spirit Communication

Carole J. Obley

A series of after-death spirit communications which uplift, comfort and heal, and show how love helps us grieve.

Paperback: 978-1-84694-107-8 ebook: 978-1-84694-639-4

Less Incomplete

A Guide to Experiencing the Human Condition Beyond the Physical Body

Sandie Gustus

Based on 40 years of scientific research, this book is a dynamic guide to understanding life beyond the physical body.

Paperback: 978-1-84694-351-5 ebook: 978-1-84694-892-3

Advanced Psychic Development

Becky Walsh

Learn how to practise as a professional, contemporary spiritual medium.

Paperback: 978-1-84694-062-0 ebook: 978-1-78099-941-8

Astral Projection Made Easy

and overcoming the fear of death

Stephanie June Sorrell

From the popular Made Easy series, *Astral Projection Made Easy* helps to eliminate the fear of death, through discussion of life beyond the physical body.

Paperback: 978-1-84694-611-0 ebook: 978-1-78099-225-9

The Miracle Workers Handbook

Seven Levels of Power and Manifestation of the Virgin Mary

Sherrie Dillard

Learn how to invoke the Virgin Mary's presence, communicate with her, receive her grace and miracles and become a miracle worker.

Paperback: 978-1-84694-920-3 ebook: 978-1-84694-921-0

Divine Guidance

The Answers You Need to Make Miracles

Stephanie J. King

Ask any question and the answer will be presented, like a direct line to higher realms… *Divine Guidance* helps you to regain control over your own journey through life.

Paperback: 978-1-78099-794-0 ebook: 978-1-78099-793-3

The End of Death

How Near-Death Experiences Prove the Afterlife

Admir Serrano

A compelling examination of the phenomena of Near-Death Experiences.

Paperback: 978-1-78279-233-8 ebook: 978-1-78279-232-1

The Psychic & Spiritual Awareness Manual

A Guide to DIY Enlightenment

Kevin West

Discover practical ways of empowering yourself by unlocking your psychic awareness, through the Spiritualist and New Age approach.

Paperback: 978-1-78279-397-7 ebook: 978-1-78279-396-0

An Angels' Guide to Working with the Power of Light

Laura Newbury

Discovering her ability to communicate with angels, Laura Newbury records her inspirational messages of guidance and answers to universal questions.

Paperback: 978-1-84694-908-1 ebook: 978-1-84694-909-8

The Audible Life Stream

Ancient Secret of Dying While Living

Alistair Conwell

The secret to unlocking your purpose in life is to solve the mystery of death, while still living.

Paperback: 978-1-84694-329-4 ebook: 978-1-78535-297-3

Beyond Photography
Encounters with Orbs, Angels and Mysterious Light Forms!
John Pickering, Katie Hall
Orbs have been appearing all over the world in recent years. This is the personal account of one couple's experience of this new phenomenon.
Paperback: 978-1-90504-790-1

Blissfully Dead
Life Lessons from the Other Side
Melita Harvey
The spirit of Janelle, a former actress, takes the reader on a fascinating and insightful journey from the mind to the heart.
Paperback: 978-1-78535-078-8 ebook: 978-1-78535-079-5

Does It Rain in Other Dimensions?
A True Story of Alien Encounters
Mike Oram
We have neighbors in the universe. This book describes one man's experience of communicating with other-dimensional and extra-terrestrial beings over a 50-year period.
Paperback: 978-1-84694-054-5

Readers of ebooks can buy or view any of these bestsellers by clicking on the live link in the title. Most titles are published in paperback and as an ebook. Paperbacks are available in traditional bookshops. Both print and ebook formats are available online.
Find more titles and sign up to our readers' newsletter at http://www.johnhuntpublishing.com/mind-body-spirit. Follow us on Facebook at https://www.facebook.com/OBooks and Twitter at https://twitter.com/obooks.